COLIN TEEVAN: TWO PLAYS

Colin Teevan

TWO PLAYS

THE BIG SEA
VINEGAR AND BROWN PAPER

OBERON BOOKS
LONDON

WWW.OBERONBOOKS.COM

First published in 2002 by Oberon Books Ltd
521 Caledonian Road, London N7 9RH
Tel: +44 (0) 20 7607 3637 / Fax: +44 (0) 20 7607 3629
e-mail: info@oberonbooks.com
www.oberonbooks.com

A catalogue record for this book is available from the British
Library.

PB ISBN: 9781840022285
E ISBN: 9781786822284

Cover design by Oberon Books
Typography by Jeff Willis
eBook conversion by Lapiz Digital Services, India.

Contents

Introduction

Jack Bradley

Under the Influences...

An Irish navvy pitches up at a building site looking for work and the foreman says:

> 'Have you done work like this before then?'
>
> 'I have, surely.'
>
> 'Then, you'll know the difference between a joist and a girder?'
>
> 'Doesn't everyone?' the navvy says, 'Sure, Joyce wrote Ulysses and Goethe did Faust.'

Jokes do more than make us laugh. As the Polish cartoonist Grock once said, every joke is a time bomb waiting to explode. A good joke strips away the veneer of gentility and respectability to reveal our prejudices and preconceptions, the contradictions that lie so often at the heart of things. And so the gag above speaks volumes, predicated, as it is, upon the premise of the stereotypic 'thick paddy' who is barely literate and invariably slow on the uptake. The joke takes this assumption on and confounds it. It reminds us of the Irish contribution to intellectual and artistic life. What astonishes is the need for the joke at all when one contemplates the scale of that contribution. Only look at the influence of the Irish on English Theatre to realise how impoverished our canon would be without the likes of Wilde, Shaw *et al.* Indeed, arguably, for the last 250 years since Sheridan bought His Majesty's Theatre at Drury Lane from Garrick, the Irish have proved a mainstay to the British Theatre scene.

But can one define or categorise that influence? And if so, where does Colin Teevan fit in? No writing exists in a vacuum and no self-respecting writer would not want to read those seminal authors who speak to the age. So writers read and they are influenced. Yet no writer wishes to be thought as derivative, but we, as critics and as an audience, often expect the wholly original. In fact, life is a moving image and the zeitgeist subtly changes and so, organically, literature alters to reflect it. I write this because to describe Teevan as subject to influence is to acknowledge the inevitable rather than challenge notions of his originality. Quite simply, he is part of a theatrical continuum.

Of course, to be Irish has changed from era to era. We associate that first influx of Irish playwrights in the eighteenth century – best exemplified by Sheridan, Farquhar, O'Keefe – with wit, charm, gaiety and brio: comic social observation the watchword. In a way, this should not surprise because Sheridan's experience typified that of Irish writers of the time. An Anglo-Irish protestant he might have been but that did not make him entirely acceptable to the English Aristocracy. To be Irish then meant one could be *in* London society but not entirely *of* it. In Wilde and Shaw over a century later one detects the same acute fascination with social mores, an unquenchable desire to dissect the phenomenon that was Victorian English Society. Subsequently both Wilde and Shaw have come to be almost adopted as English playwrights, so invisible were their national origins reflected in their work. Not for the first time, the Empire absorbed, assimilated and was enriched by its conquests.

The story is somewhat different for those who remained in Ireland. If there had always been a steady trickle of emigrants from Ireland to England – not least in the form of mercenaries as depicted by the Stage Irishman McMaurice in *Henry IV, Part II* – the transforming event of the nineteenth century was the Irish Famine. A farming country that had always put its trust in the land suddenly put its faith in flight. The great exodus began and has continued since, so that the pervading themes of migration (see Friel's *Philadephia, Here I Come*) and of homecoming (see Murphy's *Conversation on a Homecoming* or, more recently, *The Wake*) were enshrined in Irish Literature. Unsurprisingly, given the causes of the Famine and the English response to it, there emerged a new nationalism in Ireland and this was reflected in the artists' concerns and, indeed, new forms. Under Yeats and Synge there was a movement to build a new Irish playwriting aesthetic, returning to folkloric subjects, myths and classical themes. Curiously, much of this was written in English, thus prompting Flann O'Brien, in his entertainingly scurrilous essay 'It

Goes Without Synge', to opine: There is a new type of literature doing the rounds under the description Anglo-Irish literature – well, let me tell you: it is neither Anglo, Irish nor Literature! The gael-speaking O'Brien may have found this contradictory but with the emergence of Synge came, in *The Playboy of the Western World*, the coalescence of a handful of themes that have dogged Irish drama for a century. In Chrissie Mahon we have a character who yearns to be free but is trapped by an overbearing father. When he arrives in the Shebeen and announces he has murdered his father he is lionised by a community unacquainted with the stark realities of such actions. To the sleepy and unworldly village, violence has an alluring charm. Arguably, such themes came to their apotheosis in Gary Mitchell's plays which deal almost exclusively with the brutalising effect of casual violence in the Troubled North.

In this whistle-stop tour of Irish theatre there will be necessary omissions, but one cannot bypass the storytelling tradition that manifests itself in the populist, flamboyant melodrama of the countless plays of Boucicault and carried on in the twentieth century by John B Keane. In Martin McDonagh's intricately plotted Leenane tales of the remote West, Boucicault and Keane have their natural successor. Of course, storytelling comes in a variety of forms and proliferation of the small-scale studio play in recent years has led to the emergence of a genre that might be described as interlocking narrative voices, in particular the plays of Conor McPherson and Mark O'Rowe, to name but two. Of course, the original forerunner of such plays is *Faith Healer* by Friel. What categorises these new writers however is their tendency to write about the contemporary urban landscape. If the generation of Murphy and Friel concerned themselves with the issues of land, class and family break-up, the newer voices inhabit a territory where drugs, prostitution and petty crime are an everyday occurrence. But squalor and inner-city deprivation are not the prerogatives of the late twentieth century and the new realism has, as its ancestor, the work of O'Casey who, in such plays as *Juno and the Paycock* revealed a turn of the century tenement Dublin that so appalled its audiences as to have them rioting in the aisles. It was not yet a country ready to question itself in the heady cauldron of live theatre.

I think it was the poet Patrick Kavanagh said, 'All our wars were merry, all our songs are sad,' and one would be hard pressed to dispute his suggestion that there is – if it's not yet another contradiction in terms – a healthy morbidity about some Irish writing. The perennial themes of death and disease bubble lightly beneath the surface of much of Yeats, Synge, and O'Casey and, certainly, the baton has been taken up by such as Marina Carr and Sebastian Barry who, in *Portia Coghlan* and *The Bog of Cats* and *The Steward of Christendom* and *Our Lady of Sligo*, respectively, marry an unashamed lyricism to contemporary Irish writing with a sense of the transitory. However, if there is one author who has unequivocally appropriated the macabre it is Samuel Beckett. If his character Murphy has a pocketful of sucking stones, dear Samuel B had one, I suspect, brimmed full of coffin nails.

I have left Beckett until last because he is paradoxically a massive cultural influence upon Irish writers as well as being Ireland's most European son. Significantly, he was an exile, someone who did not truly find his feet until he began thinking in French. If the near garrulousness of Anglo-Irish banter has often lent endless comic potential, then the bitter-sweet absurdity of life's fleeting joys and enduring pains have somehow been best encapsulated in the brevity and clarity that French prose offers. With Beckett's arrival on the scene as a playwright, the dramatic landscape altered for a generation. It is no surprise then that he should cast a light on our understanding of Teevan's work.

For Teevan, the story really begins with *The Big Sea*, a punning title since the play is set within what we take to be a cancer ward. At least two of the protagonists, Caresme and Charnau, are diagnosed with what we take to be a terminal condition. As to the set the only specifications are three boxes. These are later used to signify the 'ships' the three patients will embark upon in their journey across the Big Sea to the New World. Of course, for boxes read coffins, for New World read the Next. We are immediately in a metaphoric world where nothing is quite to be taken at face value. Thus, time is eked out playing games: Monopoly, Scrabble and, eventually (and significantly), Trivial Pursuit. This is life as a process of passing time until the inevitable happens. Given the inmates' medical state, the play's preoccupations are with illness and death. The only respite is Christophe's vain and futile pursuit of love with Sister Innocence. He alone has yet to be diagnosed and as such is allowed some hope. But, in this world, life is a ticking clock and the repetitive visits by the medics serve only to exacerbate the sense of precious time ebbing away. All this is on the surface decidedly Beckettian, but Teevan is subject to more than one influence and he decides to play fast and loose with theatrical trick and device. With the casting of Caresme into the audience the convention of the 'fourth wall' is routinely abandoned; the ascent into the flies a *deus ex machina* in reverse; and finally with the calling of 'Maestro' to the sound department, the artifice of theatre is celebrated rather than concealed.

With *Vinegar and Brown Paper*, Teevan seems to have moved closer to a realist portrayal of life. This is contemporary Dublin and failed stand-up Jack and sculptor Jill have returned from a spell in England. Blithely we think we know where we are. This is a Homecoming play. But, of course, there is more going on. If the familiar themes of death and guilt (Jill is mourning her abandoned mother's death) are there, so are a handful of others including the artist's concerns about his/her responsibilities in portraying life. More importantly, the desire to challenge form once again is paramount. We have Jill's dream-state monologues and Jack's comedy routines, but nowhere is the formal challenge more boldly made than in the way Jack and Jill's life is mirrored by the Aussie TV soaps Jill retreats into watching. Yet again, the stage image of life imitating bad art is a wholly theatrical – and sustained – metaphor.

With *The Walls*, published separately by Oberon and presented by the Royal National Theatre in 2001, Teevan takes these theatrical experiments even further. Again it is a homecoming play, this time on Christmas Eve, with Joe returned from England where he pretends to be enjoying success life in stark contrast to his brother John, an aspirant novelist living upstairs. Success is nothing less than everyone expects. After all, the Walls are a middle-class Dublin family. But the subject of the play is not just the people but also, quite literally, the walls – that is, the bricks and mortar of their family home. The *mise-en-scene* of the play demands that the walls literally disappear, a clear theatrical metaphor for the tenuousness of their grip on reality and on their happiness. The theatrical joke is one that explodes, gentility and respectability are blown apart and the family idyll and all its hypocrisies and little secrets exposed and destroyed.

Read in the context of the plays that preceded it, this *coup de theatre* comes as no surprise. But then, Teevan is both a son of Ireland and – though he writes about the perennial concerns that have preoccupied Ireland's major dramatists: land, migration, class, death and love – at heart a European. This is best revealed by the plays that he has chosen to translate and the stories he has adapted. As a Greek-reading classicist his oeuvre has varied from a punk version of *Iphigeneia in Aulis* (*Iph…*) to work as dramaturg on Peter Hall's production of John Barton's *Tantalus* and, most recently, translator of *Bacchai* at the RNT. None can be described quite as kitchen sink.

Looking at his chosen adaptations of modern material, such as *Marathon* by Edoardo Erba or *Cuckoos* by Giuseppi Manfridi, once again one sees him gravitate towards the intrinsically theatrical. In the first we have two athletes talking as they conduct a run – a literally exhausting performance; and in the latter arguably we have a marriage of the absurdist and the classical unities. In his adaptation of Hasek's novel *Svejk* (1999) the appeal of dadaist and futurist forms comes to the fore and more recently in *Monkey* (2001), his take on the Hsi-yu Chi fairy tale, we see a blend of East meets West, of the magical, mythical and metaphysical.

So his cultural cousins are those that challenge reality in theatrical and philosophical terms – the Europeans Pirandello, Filippo and Ionesco all spring to mind. But to confine him thus is to underestimate the ever-changing influences. Quite where he will carry their baton – and the batons of others – now remains to be seen.

London, May 2002
Jack Bradley, Literary Manager
of the National Theatre, London

THE BIG SEA

for David, Theresia and their three little Cs

Characters

CHRISTOPHE

CHARNAU

CARESME

SISTER INNOCENCE

MATRON

The Big Sea was first performed on 3 August 1990 by Galloglass Theatre Company at the Abymill Theatre, Fethard, County Tipperary, Ireland, with the following cast:

CHRISTOPHE, Fergus Colville

CHARNAU, Ted Dawson

CARESME, Luke Hayden

INNOCENCE, Mary Barnes

MATRON, Nuala Walsh

Director, Simon Bayly

Designer, Theresia Guschlbauer

Lighting desiger, Richard Dixon

The Big Sea was first presented in this form as *Le Grand Large* at the Theatre de l'Odeon, Paris on 19 December 1991 and subsequently at the Chartreuse Avignon in July 1992, with the following cast:

CHRISTOPHE, Alain Libolt

CHARNAU, Christian Drillaud

CARESME, Samir Said

SISTER INNOCENCE, Cecille Pillet

INFERMIERE EN CHEF, Simone Signoret

Director, Michel Dubois

Translator, Alexandra Poulain

Scene 1: Cards

Three patients. Three boxes. CARESME is trying to hang himself on his own drip. CHARNAU reclines. CHRISTOPHE sits on his bed.

CARESME: O my God, why me?

CHARNAU: I really do respect a man who despises himself because, in despising himself, he respects himself as someone who can despise.

CHRISTOPHE: There must be something we can do.

CHARNAU: Let's face it, we're dying.

CHRISTOPHE: I'm not, I'm not dying.

CHARNAU: We're in agony, we're in mortal fear. Yet, pleasure and pain are two heads of the one animal: if we're in pain, then there must be pleasure to be found here too.

CARESME: O God, o God, why me?

CHRISTOPHE: I'm sick to death of your god.

CHARNAU: And after all, when you think about it, who isn't dying? We are all…pregnant with our own deaths.

CHRISTOPHE: I'm not, I'm alive.

CHARNAU: True, but you are also dying, else why would you be here?

CHRISTOPHE: Where?

CHARNAU: Here, this is where people die. You're dying, we're all dying.

CHRISTOPHE: But I haven't been diagnosed yet.

CHARNAU: Do you really need to be? Do you really want to be?

CHRISTOPHE: Look, do I have a tumour like yours, do I?

CHARNAU: You soon will.

CHRISTOPHE: I will not.

CHARNAU: You will too.

CHRISTOPHE: I won't.

(Another groan from CARESME.)

CHARNAU: Will you cut him down and get him to shut up?

CHRISTOPHE: You do.

CHARNAU: I can't.

CHRISTOPHE: Why not?

CHARNAU: I'm sicker than you are.

CHRISTOPHE: You are not.

CHARNAU: Look at my tumour.

CHRISTOPHE: You said I'd soon have one.

CHARNAU: Haha, you admit it, you are ill.

CARESME: O God, o God forgive me, forgive me –

CHARNAU: Listen, how can we argue in peace with this racket going on? Cut him down.
(*Pause. CHRISTOPHE does so. Silence.*)
Imminent death is a wonder, isn't it?
(*CARESME is still moaning. CHARNAU hits him.*)

CARESME: Thank you.

CHARNAU: The pleasure was all mine. As I was saying, imminent death is a wonder, it's a licence to think and do as one wants without retribution, without fear of judgement. Pure freedom. I mean, if we murder someone, who's going to bother arresting us? We'd die before the trial.

CHRISTOPHE: If death is a licence to do anything, what are we doing here, doing nothing?

CHARNAU: I don't know about you, but I'm basking in the autumn of my life.

CHRISTOPHE: Then why bring up the possibilities of what we might do, if you've no intention of doing anything?

CHARNAU: I was only saying 'if'.

CHRISTOPHE: If! If! If!

CHARNAU: We must explore 'the permanent possibility of experience.' Who said that?

CARESME: You did.

CHARNAU: Yes, I suppose I did.

CHRISTOPHE: But I want experience, not just the possibility of it.

CHARNAU: The possibility is the experience.

CARESME: Say we don't die.

CHARNAU: When?

CHRISTOPHE: When we murder someone and get arrested, say we live on and spend the rest of our days in prison?

CARESME: Our days are a prison. 'O woe to those who refuse to recognise their own wretchedness.'

CHARNAU: But we must die. They've given us no time.

CHRISTOPHE: How do 'they' know?

CHARNAU: Because they do. What do you think they're there for?

CHRISTOPHE: Where?

CARESME: He knows. 'O double woe to those who love this miserable and corruptible life.'

CHRISTOPHE: And who are 'they' anyhow?

CHARNAU: Them. The matron, the nurse. The doctors. Who else?

CARESME: The doctors have given up hope, I've heard them, I've heard them say it. What's the point in going on?

CHRISTOPHE: I haven't given up hope.

CHARNAU: But you're dying, what's the point in hoping?

CARESME: Will you stop talking about death?

CHRISTOPHE: We're not, we're talking about hope.

CHARNAU: I don't know about you, but I'm talking about death.

CHRISTOPHE: You'd like to think you knew what we were talking about.

CARESME: What are we talking about?

CHRISTOPHE: This is hopeless.

CHARNAU: See, it's hopeless, I must be right.
  (*Silence.*)
  Looks like the conversation died.
  (*Silence.*)
  I do understand you, my friend. I too was as angry and disbelieving as you once. I thought I could live forever. But I learned by bitter experience and faced up to the fact of my mortality.

CHRISTOPHE: How do you know it is a fact?

CHARNAU: My friend the doctors know. They have divined the nature of our ailment and alotted us our span. We may as well enjoy what little's left.

CARESME: Will you stop it? This conversation's killing me.
  (*MATRON enters.*)

MATRON: What seems to be the problem gentlemen?

CHARNAU: We're dying of cancer.

CARESME: Don't say that word.

CHARNAU: What word?

CARESME: 'That' word.

CHARNAU: 'That' word?

CARESME: The big 'C'.

CHARNAU: What? Cancer?

MATRON: Come, come, calm yourselves. None of you have cancer.

CHRISTOPHE: See, I told you.

MATRON: None of you are dying.

CHRISTOPHE: Told you so.

CHARNAU: None of us are dying, we're all dying, what's the difference?

MATRON: You are all ill, however.

CARESME: What do I have?

MATRON: You have lymphoma.

CHARNAU: And what do I have?

MATRON: You have a soft tissue sarcoma.

CARESME: What's that I have again?

MATRON: A lymphoma.

CARESME: That's not cancer is it?

MATRON: No, not exactly.

CARESME: I'm not going to die, am I?

MATRON: We have great hope.

CHARNAU: I'm not going to live, am I?

MATRON: For a while you shall.

CHARNAU: But I shall die some day?

MATRON: We all must.

CARESME: O God, why do you punish me?

MATRON: Calm down, please, you're all over-wrought. You've got too much time to think, sitting here, doing nothing.

CHRISTOPHE: How can you have too much time?

MATRON: A game, a nice game, that's it.

CHRISTOPHE: It's not a game, it's real.

MATRON: Come, come, do you think you're in any fit condition to know what's real and what is not?

CHRISTOPHE: I don't know what condition I'm in at all.

MATRON: A nice card game is called for to take your mind
    off –

CHRISTOPHE: Off what?

CHARNAU: Excellent idea.

    (*MATRON gives the cards to CHARNAU, who starts
    laying out a game with CARESME.*)

CHRISTOPHE: Cards?

CARESME: Deal!

    (*CHARNAU does so.*)

MATRON: I must be off, some of us have work to do.

CHRISTOPHE: Why can't we work?

MATRON: Because you're ill.

CHRISTOPHE: Why cards? Why games?

CHARNAU: I'll take two.

MATRON: They are a good diversion from your illness.

CARESME: Two nines and a two.

CHRISTOPHE: But what is my illness?

MATRON: We're awaiting tests.

CHARNAU: Full house, I win.

    (*CHARNAU collects.*)

CHRISTOPHE: But I haven't had any?

MATRON: That's what we're awaiting.

CARESME: Deal!

CHRISTOPHE: But what have I got to take my mind off, if I
    don't know whether I'm ill or not?

MATRON: We've got to take your mind off thinking you
    might be ill.

CARESME: One card.

CHARNAU: I'll take two.

CHRISTOPHE: I want to know what's going on.

MATRON: And you will just as soon as we do.

CARESME: Two nines and a two.

CHRISTOPHE: But when?

CHARNAU: A flush, I win.

    (*He collects.*)

CHRISTOPHE: When will you know?

MATRON: You must trust us. Good day.

    (*MATRON exits.*)

CARESME: Deal!

CHARNAU: Are you playing, my friend?

CHRISTOPHE: How can you play cards with all this going on?

CHARNAU: All this what?

CHRISTOPHE: All this…nothing.

CARESME: One card.

CHARNAU: I'll take two. Have we anything better to do?

CHRISTOPHE: Yes…no.

CARESME: Two nines and a two.

CHARNAU: Poker.

(*CHARNAU collects.*)

CARESME: Poker?

CHARNAU: Yes, four aces.

CARESME: But we're playing twenty-ones.

CHARNAU: No we're not.

CARESME: Yes we are.

CHARNAU: Dealer chooses, and I was playing poker.

CARESME: But you only gave me two cards.

CHARNAU: You didn't seem like you wanted any more.

CARESME: But you gave yourself five.

CHARNAU: That's because I was playing poker.

CARESME: But you only gave me two!

CHARNAU: Well you didn't say anything.

CARESME: Let me deal then.

CHARNAU: I've had enough, you play patience if you like.

CARESME: Stop talking about patients and death and illness will you?

(*Silence. CARESME starts to play patience.*)

Charnau?

CHARNAU: Yes, Caresme?

CARESME: Thanks.

CHARNAU: It's a pleasure. For what?

CARESME: The game.

CHARNAU: O yes.

CARESME: It's not every day you learn a trick like that. Some day I might be able to use it on my friends. If I ever have any.

CHARNAU: And if you weren't going to die.

CARESME: Yes.
   (*Silence.*)
   I've even lost to myself.
CHARNAU: Cheat.
CARESME: I can't.

Scene 2: The Map

CHARNAU, CARESME and CHRISTOPHE study a map.

ALL: Hmmmmm.
CARESME: Looks more like a treadmill to me.
CHARNAU: Or a large soufflé.
ALL: Hmmmm.
CARESME: Where did it come from?
CHRISTOPHE: I don't know.
CHARNAU: And you don't know what it is exactly?
CHRISTOPHE: No.
ALL: Hmmmm.
CHRISTOPHE: I do remember, it's a map.
CARESME: Of what?
CHRISTOPHE: An old man.
CHARNAU: An old man?
CHRISTOPHE: A story an old man told me. It's of the
   world, both that which is known and that which is as yet
   unknown. This old man, a sailor, he told me he had been
   travelling between Britain and Spain and was blown off
   course. He talked of a new world brimming with wealth
   and fertile land.
CHARNAU: Wealth you say?
CHRISTOPHE: Yes, a miraculous land, a garden brimming
   with fruit, untouched by civilised man.
CHARNAU: And you drew a map of how to get to this place?
   Let's have another look then.
ALL: Hmmmm.
CHARNAU: I still think it looks like a large soufflé, or maybe
   a trifle. Hell, it could be anything.
CHRISTOPHE: In that case could it not be here, this ward,
   as much as anything else?

CARESME: But you said it was a map of a new world.

(*CHRISTOPHE starts to re-arrange the room.*)

CHARNAU: Did the old man not say anything else?

CHRISTOPHE: Yes, it's round.

CARESME: Our world?

CHARNAU: I told you.

CHRISTOPHE: He said our world is round and that if one travels west for sixty-eight degrees, the chains of the big sea will break apart and a vast and mighty kingdom shall be revealed.

CHARNAU: Wealthy, you say?

CHRISTOPHE: Boundlessly.

CARESME: Man should not tempt the almighty by seeking the unknown depths of the ocean. It might be flat and we'll fall off the edge of the world. He said the map looked like this ward, and that's flat. We shall fall off and be eaten by dragons.

CHARNAU: Like this ward you say, and wealthy, very wealthy?

CHRISTOPHE: Unlimited wealth.

CHARNAU: That's good enough for me. Do you think we could make the crossing from here?

CARESME: It's flat, flat as this ward, we'll fall off and die.

CHRISTOPHE: Yes, yes I suppose we could.

CARESME: We'll perish on the high seas. We'll sail into the abyss.

CHARNAU: Listen my friend, this map here is flat like this ward, correct?

CARESME: Correct.

CHARNAU: This map is of a round world, correct?

CARESME: Correct.

CHARNAU: Therefore this flat ward is a round world. QED.

CARESME: (*Falling to knees.*) O my God.

CHARNAU: (*To CHRISTOPHE.*) Now I must invest you as admiral of the fleet.

(*CHRISTOPHE kneels while CHARNAU invests him.*) And by this my patent, I give you all power completely; that you might exercise civil and criminal jurisdiction in both granting letters of marque and deciding in all disputes that may happen on the sea.

CHRISTOPHE: Lend me the use of three caravels and
    I shall find this new world for you, this garden of paradise.
CARESME: Why tempt fate?
CHRISTOPHE: Fate does not exist, we write our own
    destinies. Follow me, men, and you shall not go in
    darkness.

Scene 3: The Farce

*CHARNAU and CARESME are asleep. MATRON performs a
test on CHRISTOPHE.*

CHRISTOPHE: You leave me in darkness.
MATRON: We ourselves are still in the dark.
CHRISTOPHE: But I am convinced you're keeping
    something from me.
MATRON: And I am convinced you'll find nothing but grief
    if you continue to work yourself up like this. You're in no
    fit condition –
CHRISTOPHE: But what condition am I in?
MATRON: I cannot say.
CHRISTOPHE: Then let me leave.
MATRON: Where to?
CHRISTOPHE: You're doing all my thinking for me.
MATRON: What makes you think that you can think?
CHRISTOPHE: But it's been weeks, months, an age since
    you took the first tests – and still you don't know?
MATRON: We don't want to rush to any conclusions.
CHRISTOPHE: But I have the right to know what's going on.
MATRON: Well if you really want to know… The slides of
    your first test were taken for histological analysis in the
    pathological-anatomy department. They found the white/
    red blood cell count and the cellular formation to be of an
    irregular type. The histological analyst and the anatomical
    pathologist, having discussed it with the oncologist and the
    gynaecologist –
CHRISTOPHE: Gynaecologist?
MATRON: Yes, the anatomical pathologist and the
    gynaecologist are great friends, they're the hospital

foursomes champions. Anyway, the oncologist suggested on ratification from the radiologist, that a second biopsy be taken for histological analysis so that the findings of the first test might be verified or refuted.

CHRISTOPHE: But what were the findings of the first test?

MATRON: We're not quite sure, that's why we need the second test.

CHRISTOPHE: I see.

MATRON: Now the oncologist, the radiologist, the pathologist, the histologist and the chiropodist all agree that we must be sure exactly what the problem is before we commence treatment. *Medecine est lucis ortu nunc et in perpetuum.* You must trust us.

(*Pause.*)

CHRISTOPHE: But when can I know?

MATRON: When we know.

CHRISTOPHE: But when shall that be?

MATRON: Is it so important *when?*

CHRISTOPHE: Yes.

MATRON: Why?

CHRISTOPHE: There are things I must do before –

MATRON: Before what?

CHRISTOPHE: Before I die.

MATRON: Who's dying?

CHRISTOPHE: We all die.

MATRON: But not quite yet. You must hope for the best. You must put your faith in us.

CHRISTOPHE: But if I have got…if I am dying, you cannot save me, you cannot alter fate, you cannot help me find –

MATRON: Find what?

CHRISTOPHE: Answers.

MATRON: What answers?

CHRISTOPHE: To questions.

MATRON: To what questions?

CHRISTOPHE: I cannot die without ever having looked, even if I fail.

MATRON: But looked for what?

CHRISTOPHE: How do I know? I haven't looked yet.

MATRON: You're over-excited, you must be looking for
    something.

CHRISTOPHE: (*Exasperated.*) …expression.

MATRON: Of what?

CHRISTOPHE: I don't know.

MATRON: You're in a fever.

CHRISTOPHE: I'm not.

MATRON: Expression of what?

CHRISTOPHE: I *don't know.*

MATRON: You're being hysterical.

CHRISTOPHE: I'm not.

MATRON: Then what are you looking to express?

CHRISTOPHE: I cannot say.

MATRON: You're growing delirious.

CHRISTOPHE: I am not feverish, delirious, psychotic
    or hysterical. I am not schizoid, paranoid, manic or
    neurotic. I do not have a fever, an ague, leishmaniasis,
    bilharzia, hookworm, trachoma, glaucoma, riverblindness,
    yaws, leprosy, beri-beri or kwashiorkor. There is something
    wrong and I want to know what.
    (*Pause.*)
    It is not a question of what the sickness is called or who
    diagnoses it, it is a question of how long. I want to know
    how soon. I want to… I want to find what I cannot name
    because I've never known it. To find love, to express love,
    to feel love before I die.
    (*Silence.*)

MATRON: Is that all?

CHRISTOPHE: Is that *all?!*

MATRON: You must have known love before, everyone has.

CHRISTOPHE: I have not.

MATRON: Has there never been a girl you loved or cared
    for?

CHRISTOPHE: I don't remember any. If there was I've
    forgotten her.

MATRON: Your mother. You must have loved your mother,
    or she must have loved you?

CHRISTOPHE: I didn't have a mother.

MATRON: You must have.

CHRISTOPHE: I don't remember any.

MATRON: Someone must have given birth to you.

CHRISTOPHE: No one did. I did. Perhaps I have not yet been born.

MATRON: Of course you were born. It's a medical impossibility not to have been.

CHRISTOPHE: I tell you I wasn't.

MATRON: As sure as God is watching me you were.

CHRISTOPHE: How can you be sure God is watching you?

MATRON: What?

CHRISTOPHE: How can you be sure? How do you know he's there?

MATRON: Because he is.

CHRISTOPHE: Is what?

MATRON: He who is. Because we are here.

CHRISTOPHE: Where?

MATRON: Because the sun shines and the great sea pitches and rolls –

(*SISTER INNOCENCE enters and injects CHRISTOPHE.*)

CHRISTOPHE: (*Deliriously.*) I hear the big sea rolls and yearns and craves, but I do too. I must find it, look for it. (*Pause.*)

Sister?

INNOCENCE: Sir?

MATRON: Sister?

CHRISTOPHE: Sister…

INNOCENCE: Sir…?

CHRISTOPHE: Sister.

MATRON: Mister! Sister!

(*CHRISTOPHE passes out.*)

Scene 4: Monopoly

CHARNAU, CARESME and CHRISTOPHE are playing Monopoly.

CHARNAU: Your turn.

CARESME: (*Throws dice.*) Three and four. One, two, three, four, five, six, seven, eight.

CHARNAU: (*Consults card.*) That's mine I believe…with two hotels…that's eighteen hundred you owe me.

CARESME: But they're houses, they're green. They're not hotels, hotels are red.

CHARNAU: Green! Red! What do you know? I once sailed with an Irishman who had Alzheimer's disease and it impaired his sight. On St. Patrick's Day he put on a pair of what he thought were green socks but they were really red and he went along to the galley where all the Irish Americans were celebrating. He told them that he was wearing the socks in honour of his saint's day. They thought he was referring to Karl Marx and, being American, they beat him up and threw him out. As they were doing so they said: 'That will teach you to wear red socks on St. Patrick's Day.' So he went back to his room and put on a pair of what he thought were red socks, thinking they'd be green socks, but they were in fact blue socks. On his way back to the galley he met an Englishman who thumped him in the face and threw him overboard.

CARESME: Why should an Englishman throw him overboard for wearing blue socks?

CHARNAU: It had nothing to do with the socks, the Englishman just hated the Irish.

CARESME: But what's all this to do with the game?

CHARNAU: Everything. You shouldn't trust yourself to know what is green and what is not because you're bound to make a balls of it. How do you know you haven't spent your whole life calling what's green red and what's red green?

CARESME: Maybe I have.

CHARNAU: Your houses are green, mine are red. It's good marketing strategy to offer customers a selection. I thought these large red blocks a bit anonymous for hotels, I prefer the more intimate green ones.

CARESME: But you're cheating. You bought your hotels for the same price as your houses.

CHARNAU: That's not cheating, that's good property speculation.

CARESME: I see. Shall I write you another IOU?

CHARNAU: That would do nicely. (*To CHRISTOPHE.*) Your go.

CHRISTOPHE: I'm in jail.

CHARNAU: Try for doubles.

CHRISTOPHE: Why should I? It's nice and quiet here. I've time to reflect.

CHARNAU: But that's not what the game is about.

CHRISTOPHE: But what's the point in getting out of jail? You own everything, I'm safer here.

CHARNAU: That's not in the spirit of the game. You should play to the end.

CHRISTOPHE: But where does it end?

CHARNAU: When somebody wins.

CHRISTOPHE: But when will that be? What's the point in these games?

CHARNAU: Passes the time.

CHRISTOPHE: Is our time so worthless, that it must be filled in?

CARESME: There's so much of it, it must be disposed of.

CHARNAU: It's that there's too little, it must be enjoyed.

(*CHRISTOPHE hits the game board.*)

CHRISTOPHE: What's the point? Tell me, what's the point?

CHARNAU: Matron! Matron!

(*They struggle over the board. The MATRON enters.*)

MATRON: The point, if you must know, is that games are a good metaphor for life. There are all the joys and sorrows of winning and losing. The cut and thrust of business.

CHARNAU: The pleasures and responsibilities of home ownership.

MATRON: (*Picks up a game piece.*) Having a car.

CARESME: (*Ditto.*) Having a shoe.

CHRISTOPHE: I don't want a metaphor, I want life!

MATRON: Come, come, what is this life you speak of if it isn't these things?

CHRISTOPHE: It's, it's –

CHARNAU: It's home ownership.

CARESME: Having another shoe.

CHRISTOPHE: No, no, no! (*He threatens to upset the board again.*)

MATRON: Sister! Sister! Some medication, quickly!

CHRISTOPHE: No, it's okay. I just wanted to know. (*CHRISTOPHE sits down dejected. MATRON waves SISTER INNOCENCE away. When all is calmed down, she returns to her seat. Pause.*)

CARESME: How did they know it was Alzheimer's Disease?

CHARNAU: Who?

CARESME: Well, if the Irishman drowned before he found out he had Alzheimer's, how did anyone else know he had it?

CHARNAU: Simple. He didn't drown. From the autopsy it transpired that he died of a heart attack. Since, as you will remember, he saw red as blue, similarly he saw blue as red, he thought he'd fallen into a sea of blood and died of the shock.

CARESME: I see. (*Pause.*)

Scene 5: The Farce

CARESME and CHARNAU sleep. SISTER INNOCENCE, doing her rounds, attempts to give CHRISTOPHE sleeping tablets.

CHRISTOPHE: I said no.

INNOCENCE: But you must.

CHRISTOPHE: No.

INNOCENCE: It's your medication.

CHRISTOPHE: You don't even know what's wrong with me yet.

INNOCENCE: It's to keep you stable.

CHRISTOPHE: Am I a horse?

INNOCENCE: What?

CHRISTOPHE: What kind of medication is it?

INNOCENCE: I don't know. It was prescribed. My job is to make sure –

CHRISTOPHE: Prescribed by who?

INNOCENCE: The doctors.

CHRISTOPHE: What doctors?

INNOCENCE: You must take it.

CHRISTOPHE: Why?

INNOCENCE: You'll feel better.

CHRISTOPHE: I want to be better, not *feel* better.

INNOCENCE: You will be better if you take this.

CHRISTOPHE: I won't, I'll feel sleepy and stupid. I'll believe anything I'm told. I'll believe…you.

INNOCENCE: Please take it.

(*CHRISTOPHE takes it. Pause. Then swallows it.*)

CHRISTOPHE: What is your name?

INNOCENCE: Sister Innocence.

CHRISTOPHE: What a sweet name, it sounds like…well, just like…like innocence.

(*CARESME and CHARNAU groan simultaneously in their sleep.*)

INNOCENCE: What is your name?

CHRISTOPHE: Christophe.

INNOCENCE: That means bearer of Christ.

CHRISTOPHE: Of who?

INNOCENCE: Christ.

CHRISTOPHE: (*Drowsily.*) O.

INNOCENCE: Yes, St Christopher was a tall strong pagan who yearned to know Christ but did not know how to find him. He lived by the bank of a river in Asia. On this river there was a dangerous ford and because he was so strong he used to carry many travellers across the river. One day he heard a child cry out, 'Christopher, carry me across the river.' So he took the infant on his shoulders but as he waded across the river, the child's weight increased so that it was all Christopher could do to keep his head above water. Eventually, however, they reached the other side in safety. He set the child down and said, 'You have put me in great danger for your burden became so great, it's as if I carried the whole world upon my shoulders,' and the child replied –

CHRISTOPHE: Your eyes, mysterious continents –

INNOCENCE: Marvel not, said the child, for you have born
upon your back the whole world and he who created it.
I am the child who you have served every time you have
born a traveller across the river. Plant your staff near your
cabin and tomorrow your garden shall burgeon forth with
flowers and fruit. I am your lord and saviour –

CHRISTOPHE: – They flash and flicker like candle flames,
like white waves reflecting the moon. Look at me. Look at
me. (*He yawns.*) Let me read of golden lands the writers of
old describe, where people could live simply without lies
or laws or libel, content to satisfy nature.
(*He yawns.*) Look at me just this once, I am –

INNOCENCE: Please don't say you are.

CHRISTOPHE: I am, I must be. Let me look at you, your
beauty, your health –

INNOCENCE: Sleep.

CHRISTOPHE: No, let me stay a while more in the light.
I must find the words to – (*He yawns.*) – flashing, yearning,
like white waves. Innocence – (*He yawns.*) …they named
you well.

INNOCENCE: Sleep.
(*He does.*)

Scene 6: Setting Sail

The three boxes as three ships. CHRISTOPHE is the Admiral,
CHARNAU the pilot and CARESME the entire crew.

CHARNAU: Sleepy are you? I'll give you sleepy. Weigh
anchor you good for nothing sailor!

CARESME: (*Bewildered.*) What? Where?

CHARNAU: Spread the canvas, boy, we're going to make our
fortune. We're leaving port.

CARESME: What do you mean?

CHARNAU: Top-sail first.

CARESME: But which is which?

CHARNAU: Mainsail next. Now the foresail. Shake a leg,
crew, we don't have much time.

CARESME: But which? Where? How?

CHARNAU: Hard-a-starboard! Hard-a-starboard, I said boatswain.

(*They are moving.*)

CARESME: My God, we're moving. Forgive them, they know not what they do.

CHARNAU: Hurry up with the rigging, there's a westerly blowing from beyond the headland. Any sign of the island yet?

CHRISTOPHE: We haven't cleared port yet.

CHARNAU: Just checking. Steady as she goes, helmsman.

CHRISTOPHE: Now run before the wind, run before the wind. We'll catch the Trade Winds west of the Azores, Pilot, they'll carry us across the Tropic of Cancer.

CARESME: Don't mention that word.

CHARNAU: What? Tropic?

CARESME: No, the big 'C'.

CHARNAU: Pretty difficult for a sailor not to mention the big sea.

CARESME: O my God, it's flat, I know it is. We're going to fall off, I know it. O God, don't let me die.

CHARNAU: Victuals.

CARESME: What?

CHARNAU: Victuals! Grub! What provisions did you bring, ship's cook?

CARESME: Well, there's my dinner.

CHARNAU: (*Grabbing it.*) That will do nicely. (*Eating.*) You know, the belly is the reason man does not take himself for a god. Keep a westerly course there.

CARESME: Gibraltar!

CHRISTOPHE: The pillars of Hercules, the gateway to infinity.

CARESME: O my God, we're going to fall off, I know we are.

CHRISTOPHE: On, run on.

CHARNAU: Keep the course steady there helmsman.

CHRISTOPHE: Run with the wind, pitch past cities, towns and continents.

CHARNAU: You're sure there's wealth there?

CHRISTOPHE: Abundant.

CARESME: You're sure it's round?

CHRISTOPHE: As an orange. Rush on, break through the waves.

CHARNAU: Trim the sails, boatswain, trim the sails. Keep it steady.

CARESME: The Azores.

CHRISTOPHE: Fly on, run with the Trades, run with the Trade Winds.

CHARNAU: And there's fertile land, to own and cultivate?

CHRISTOPHE: The mangoes taste like sunsets, the coconuts taste like the clear blue sea and the passion fruit tastes like the first kiss you ever had.

CARESME: What's a kiss?

CHRISTOPHE: Look!

CHARNAU: A streak of fire –

CARESME: A bolt from the skies.

CHARNAU: It can't be more than a few leagues off.

CHRISTOPHE: Land ho at five leagues distance!

CARESME: Gloria in excelsis deo.

CHARNAU: Gloria! Gloria!

CHRISTOPHE: The new world. Sail on as fast as you can. Catch it while it's there.

CHARNAU: (*Whipping CARESME.*) Let her race, boy, let her race.

(*They all stand expectantly. Nothing.*)

CARESME: There's nothing there.

CHARNAU: A trick of the light.

CARESME: A mirage.

CHRISTOPHE: An illusion.

(*Beat.*)

It's gone.

CHARNAU: Gone.

CARESME: We're going to die, starve to death, or drown, or drop into hell and be devoured by seven-headed dragons.

CHRISTOPHE: Be quiet. Sail on. West by south-west. Keep a steady course.

CARESME: But how can you be sure there's something there?

CHRISTOPHE: Trust me.

CARESME: Some foolish story a mad old man told you. Why should we trust you?

CHRISTOPHE: I am convinced we can find it.

Scene 7: The Farce

CARESME, CHRISTOPHE and CHARNAU exercise. SISTER INNOCENCE monitors them as they do so.

INNOCENCE: You can't be.

CHRISTOPHE: But I am.

INNOCENCE: You're feverish.

CHRISTOPHE: I'm not. Believe me, it's true.

INNOCENCE: Please don't mention it again.

CHRISTOPHE: Why?

INNOCENCE: Because…it confuses me.

CHRISTOPHE: But –

INNOCENCE: Let me run these tests, that's what I'm here to do. Bend over.

CHRISTOPHE: How much more of my blood will you have to drink before you know anymore?

INNOCENCE: I'm told yours is a difficult case.

CHRISTOPHE: But when will the testing end?

INNOCENCE: We're still not sure what the trouble is.

CHRISTOPHE: But it's obvious; once there was light, now the darkness is approaching.

INNOCENCE: Lazarus thought he was dying but he wasn't.

CHRISTOPHE: Lazarus wasn't dying, he had a God as his doctor. I don't. That's why, that's why I must love before I die. I cannot love death. I cannot love something I cannot touch. I must love you. I do love you. You are life.

INNOCENCE: You don't know me.

CHRISTOPHE: I do know you, Innocence. Your beauty shone like a light through the dullness of my days.

INNOCENCE: Beauty, o please let me be.

CHRISTOPHE: You are all beauty and your beauty is your not knowing it.

INNOCENCE: Then you are destroying this beauty by uttering it. It is too transitory to be relied upon.

CHRISTOPHE: It must be grasped before it's gone.

INNOCENCE: Please, the glory of this world fades swiftly. Love must be returned and I cannot love you.

CHRISTOPHE: You must. I have seen it. I have seen you. I cannot unsee you.

INNOCENCE: It is unfair to lay the blame on me. (*She has to fight off his advances.*)

CHRISTOPHE: I love you Innocence.

INNOCENCE: It's a passing phase.

CHRISTOPHE: So's my life.

INNOCENCE: It's a momentary passion.

CHRISTOPHE: Like my life. Let me love you.

INNOCENCE: I can't.

CHRISTOPHE: Your beauty is my light.

INNOCENCE: Then you will soon be blinded.

CHRISTOPHE: But I love you.

INNOCENCE: It's an illusion.

CHRISTOPHE: It's real. Real as you and me.

INNOCENCE: I can't, please believe me. I can't love you and you must not love me. What can I say to make you believe me?

CHRISTOPHE: Say?… Say you have another lover.

INNOCENCE: But that is what I'm saying, there is another.

CHRISTOPHE: What? There is another? Who? Who could love you more than me? Who?

INNOCENCE: A man for whom I would gladly cut myself to pieces body and soul for to show the joy I feel at the pain my love for him causes me. I would undergo any torment with delight for him but still –

CHRISTOPHE: What?

INNOCENCE: But still that would not be enough. I long to be all one tongue with which to praise him, yet his magnificence makes my every word a useless folly. There is no place on this earth where my love for him can be appeased. My soul is in exile for him.

CHRISTOPHE: What kind of animal is he that he does not see your beauty? Your perfection?

INNOCENCE: O please, you know not what you say.

CHRISTOPHE: I do, I see it all too clearly. Some monster has played on your sweetness, your angelic naivety and captured you, making a caged bird of a soaring heart. My only hope is gone. Let me at him, let me rip him limb from limb. Let me tear out his heart of stone and kick it to kingdom come.

INNOCENT: Please, Christophe –

CHRISTOPHE: No, I'll not be limited anymore. I'll not be controlled. Why should I contain this bitterness any longer. Tell me who it is, tell me – !

(*CHRISTOPHE grabs her and starts shaking her. She grabs whatever large medical instrument might be to hand and hits him on the head with it. He is knocked out.*)

INNOCENCE: O, forgive me. The wounds of man inflicted on man, your wounds. When I think of the pain you endured, my breath, my body fails me. I can hardly stir for love of you. I see almost nothing. I hear but do not understand. O, those deep down torrents of your love. Take me to you and let me be yours.

Scene 8: Storm

The boxes are ships. A storm.

CHRISTOPHE: Blow zephyr, let me be yours.

CHARNAU: Gust.

CARESME: Gale.

CHRISTOPHE: Blast torrent. Flash. Gash.

CARESME: O my God, why me? Forgive me but I can't stand this, this uncertainty.

CHRISTOPHE: Sea, great monster mastering me.

CARESME: Let me die back in the ward.

CHARNAU: Stop being hysterical, you're giving me a headache.

CARESME: I'm not being hysterical. O my God, why me? Why me?

CHRISTOPHE: Bellow glorious thunder.

CHARNAU: Keep the course steady, crew.

CARESME: What course? What way are we facing? We're lost.

CHARNAU: Run with the wind.

CARESME: What wind? It's a whirlwind. 'And a third of the world will turn to blood.' We'll be eaten by dragons.

CHRISTOPHE: I was born from the teeth of dragons. Spark sea, black waves come do your damnedest.

CHARNAU: (*Losing patience, he beats CARESME.*) Trim the sails, boy, secure the rigging.

CARESME: They'll not take this hurricane.

CHARNAU: Then row, crew, row us to the new world.

CARESME: I can't, please forgive me. Don't hit me. (*He is hit.*) O my God, my illness makes me as heavy as death. (*CARESME is beaten severely by CHARNAU.*) Thank you, thank you. I knew this would happen to me. When I was young my grandfather sat me on his knee and said to me, 'One day, son, when you're a big strong man, and you've got a car and a nice house and a beautiful wife and three lovely kids, you're going to die.' O God, he was right. Why didn't I listen to him?

CHARNAU: Shut up and row, you useless lump of flesh – (*A sudden squall.*)

CHRISTOPHE: It's you. It's you she's in love with. She said she'd gladly cut herself to pieces body and soul to show the joy she feels at the pain you cause her. Every woman loves a fascist, they say. It's you.

CHARNAU: What is, my capitaine?

CHRISTOPHE: You're the monster. You're the one who's ravished her, raped her beauty. You'd make a whore of the whole world and still you'd not be satisfied.

CHARNAU: Why thank you, but to what do you specifically refer?

CHRISTOPHE: To you. You have destroyed her. You'd drag anything down to your pit of hell, even the most artless of angels –

CARESME: We have tempted the almighty, the sea is yawning wide for us. We shall die.

CHARNAU: But what are we talking about?

CHRISTOPHE: Innocence! Innocence! You have ravished and corrupted my Innocence.
(*Pause.*)
CHARNAU: Me? Yes. Why not? What was your innocence but a fallacy ripe for the pricking.
CHRISTOPHE: Phallus? Pricking?
CHARNAU: Yes, why not?
CHRISTOPHE: You mean it is you?
CHARNAU: Innocence loves me. She loves me because I put her out of the misery of her purity. I am the death of her. Innocence sneaks into my bed at night and begs me to pillage every corner of her virgin lands. You see, I am hard cold pleasurable reality for her.
CHRISTOPHE: O my Innocence, how can this be?
CARESME: Innocence? Innocence? I once had innocence.
CHRISTOPHE: What? You too?
CARESME: O I felt her touch many a time.
CHRISTOPHE: Her and you?
CARESME: But I tortured my innocence and now she tortures me. O God, why do you tantalise me so?
CHRISTOPHE: You too, then man's malice is a wrecking storm.
(*Storm.*)
Has all the world dined upon my Innocence? Has every man eaten of her? Come let the tempests and typhoons lick my bones clean. Let me sleep, let me sleep. I am weary of these winds.
(*Pause. Storm.*)
CARESME: Christophe?
(*Pause. Storm.*)
Christophe?
(*Pause. Storm.*)
Christophe?
CHRISTOPHE: What?
CARESME: Tell me again what this new world looks like?
CHRISTOPHE: No.
CARESME: Please.
CHRISTOPHE: I don't know anymore.

CARESME: Please tell me.

CHRISTOPHE: Let me sleep, let me be.

CARESME: I can't go on unless I know.

> (*Pause.*)

CHRISTOPHE: It's a garden. It was once a garden of fruitless soil, abounding in weeds, much like the land we came from. But the weeds died and plants grew in their place. The barren soil was made fertile by the tropical rains. The garden was cared for by natives who asked no more of it than sustenance. It soon became an orchard, then the trees grew heavy with blossom and the orchard became a forest and – I don't know – I'm not sure anymore. The farther I sail, the more I am afraid, unsure, we are dreaming. We are rooted to the old world. Does it matter where we die. Let me sleep.

CARESME: You must be sure. You cannot let me down.

CHRISTOPHE: My only chance of love has been destroyed. It was my only surety.

CHARNAU: Keep the course steady. These lands exist. We shall get there. On, swim on if necessary.

CARESME: O Lord, wash away my life with your flood.

CHRISTOPHE: Canvas, compass, keel and wheel are useless now. Embrace me widow-making, unchilding, unfathering sea.

Scene 9: Scrabble

The patients play scrabble. CHARNAU keeps score.

CARESME: G-O-D. God. Five points.

CHARNAU: A dog is worth twice your god.

CARESME: How?

CHARNAU: Dog. God backwards. Over a double word score.

CARESME: O. Yes. D-O-G. Dog. Ten points.

CHARNAU: Well done. You're learning. Your go, Christophe.

CHRISTOPHE: (*Points to the board.*) *I*, that's my word.

CHARNAU: That's not a word.

CHRISTOPHE: *I* is a word.

CHARNAU: That's not grammar.

CHRISTOPHE: What?

CHARNAU: I am a word.

CHRISTOPHE: Well, you just admitted it. I am a word – one point.

CHARNAU: But you can't be a word, you're a proper name, proper names aren't allowed.

(*Pause.*)

CHRISTOPHE: F-R-E-E-D-O-M. Freedom. Twenty-nine points.

CHARNAU: That's not a word.

CHRISTOPHE: Yes it is.

CHARNAU: What does it mean?

CHRISTOPHE: It means…it means being able to do what you want…being able to come and go as you will… being free.

CHARNAU: You don't even know what it means.

CHRISTOPHE: I do.

CHARNAU: You don't. This 'freedom' of yours doesn't exist.

CHRISTOPHE: Yes it does.

CHARNAU: Where?

CHRISTOPHE: Everywhere.

CHARNAU: Here?

CHRISTOPHE: Yes.

CHARNAU: Go on, show me then.

(*CHRISTOPHE attempts to find a way out. He cannot. He panics. He sits down.*)

CHRISTOPHE: You're right. It doesn't exist.

(*CHARNAU removes CHRISTOPHE's tiles.*)

CHARNAU: You forfeit your turn. My go. Q-U-I-L-L-E-T-S. Quillets on a triple word score, that's seventeen points by three, fifty-one, plus a fifty point bonus for a seven letter word and dogs trebled, that's eighteen, plus one hundred and one. One hundred and nineteen points for me. (*To CARESME.*) Your go.

CHRISTOPHE: Quillets?

CHARNAU: The plural of quillet.

CHRISTOPHE: What is a quillet?

CHARNAU: A quillet is a trick in an argument.

CHRISTOPHE: Prove it exists.

CHARNAU: I just did. (*To CARESME.*) Your go.

CARESME: C-A-N. Can. Five points.

CHARNAU: (*Looks at CARESME's letters.*) You've got
C-E-R. You could make –

CARESME: I know but I don't want to.

CHARNAU: But it's worth twice as much as your *Can.*

CARESME: Like I said, I don't want to.

CHARNAU: But –

CARESME: Will you not let me lose in peace? I don't know
the word, it doesn't exist.

CHARNAU: But it is a word, it does exist.

CARESME: Yes.

CHARNAU: And your 'cancer' is worth twenty points on a
double word score.

CARESME: Okay, you win.

CHARNAU: I usually do.

MATRON: (*Entering.*) Can I have a word with you
Christophe?

CHRISTOPHE: Not more tests.

MATRON: You'll be glad to hear that the testing is over.

CHRISTOPHE: Does that mean I can go home?

MATRON: Home?

CHRISTOPHE: Home.

(*Silence.*)

MATRON: Dear me no. No, no, no, no, no. It means we can
start to tackle your, your problem.

CHRISTOPHE: What is my problem?

MATRON: Your second biopsy confirmed the pathologist's
and histological analysts suspicions concerning the first
and after due consideration with the oncologist and the
radiologist and the psychiatrist – the psychiatrist is the
nephew of the gynaecologist whom you will remember
is a great friend of the pathologist – their first suspicions
concerning the irregular cellular formation and red/white
blood cell count were confirmed by the second opinion, so
to speak, with the result that we can commence treatment.

CHRISTOPHE: For what?

MATRON: My, my my, we are inquisitive. Well, I suppose
you must know eventually. Lie down on your bed please.

Nurse, the screen.

(*SISTER INNOCENCE enters with a screen which she puts around CHRISTOPHE and the MATRON. Sounds are heard. The screen is removed. CHRISTOPHE now has a tumour.*)

As you can see, the diagnosis is quite accurate. In the long run, it's better to be safe than sorry.

CHRISTOPHE: Well I'm sorry now.

MATRON: We're all sorry, but at least we can begin treatment.

CHRISTOPHE: So now you mutilate me?

MATRON: We are trying to save you.

CHRISTOPHE: Do I have no choice about the manner of my salvation?

MATRON: What would you know about your salvation? Besides, you've given your consent.

CHRISTOPHE: When?

MATRON: On admission.

CHRISTOPHE: I admitted nothing.

MATRON: You must rejoin the game. Take your mind off your illness.

CHARNAU: You see, my friend, I was right, you are dying. It's good you know. Sit back and enjoy what's left of, of death.

Scene 10: The Farce

SISTER INNOCENCE enters. She administers treatment.

INNOCENCE: Treatment.

CHRISTOPHE: Treatment?

INNOCENCE: Treatment.

CHRISTOPHE: What is the point?

INNOCENCE: To get better.

CHRISTOPHE: Better than what?

INNOCENCE: Do not despair.

CHRISTOPHE: What can save me now?

INNOCENCE: You shall be saved if you listen.

CHRISTOPHE: You could save me, Innocence.

INNOCENCE: No.

CHRISTOPHE: Leave your lover, whichever one.

INNOCENCE: What? Never.

CHRISTOPHE: Why not?

INNOCENCE: He's my master, he's my life.

CHRISTOPHE: Come to the New World, you can be master of your own life.

INNOCENCE: You can never be master of you own life.

CHRISTOPHE: I am. I make my own way.

INNOCENCE: Who has not passed this way before? Besides, what have you found? You're always looking, but you never find. You're afraid of what you might find.

CHRISTOPHE: I'm not. I've found you. I'm not afraid of you. Leave your lovers.

INNOCENCE: Lov*ers?*

CHRISTOPHE: Your lovers. They're monsters –

INNOCENCE: What?

CHRISTOPHE: Monsters, defilers and thieves. Two thieves.

INNOCENCE: My lover is no thief.

CHRISTOPHE: They are, they've stolen you.

INNOCENCE: They? No. He's he who is not a thief.

> (*CHRISTOPHE is now held in cruciform between the other two.*)

CHRISTOPHE: Who?

INNOCENCE: He who is.

CHRISTOPHE: Is what?

INNOCENCE: The son of man. He who suffered the pain of death. I dare not pronounce his name.

CHRISTOPHE: I am a son of man. I'm suffering the pain of death. You love me.

INNOCENCE: No, please stop.

CHRISTOPHE: It's me, it's me.

INNOCENCE: No.

CHRISTOPHE: Who then?

INNOCENCE: Him.

CHRISTOPHE: But who for Christ's sake?

INNOCENCE: Him. Jesus Christ.

CHRISTOPHE: Christ?

INNOCENCE: Christ! (*She injects him.*)

CHRISTOPHE: (*In pain.*) Jesus Christ!
INNOCENCE: Jesus Christ.
CHRISTOPHE: Jesus Christ!
INNOCENCE: O my saviour.
CHRISTOPHE: O my God.
INNOCENCE: My God.
CHRISTOPHE: Jesus Christ!
INNOCENCE: My Lord.
CHRISTOPHE: Good God.
INNOCENCE: My love.
CHRISTOPHE: But he's dead.
INNOCENCE: He lives in me. When I think of the sweat and the affliction of that poor body.
CHRISTOPHE: When I think of those legs, those breasts, the waist. The waste!
INNOCENCE: If only I could have wiped away the sweat and tears.
CHRISTOPHE: I am lost.
INNOCENCE: Forsaken through his love of man.
CHRISTOPHE: Will this torment never end?
INNOCENCE: Three days of torment for our sins.
     (*CHRISTOPHE falls to the ground.*)
     The pains my love endured for fallen man.

Scene 11: Becalmed

The three patients sit on their boxes, they are adrift. CHRISTOPHE has been staring vacantly into the middle distance. CHARNAU sings 'Row, row, row your boat' repeatedly to himself.

CARESME: What have I done to deserve this?
CHARNAU: It's still your turn at the watch.
CARESME: It's always my turn.
CHARNAU: Maybe that's why we're going round in circles.
CARESME: What am I to look out for? There's nothing but sea.
CHARNAU: You are to watch for the wind.
CARESME: You can't see the wind.
CHARNAU: Yes you can.

CARESME: How? Where? Can you see any wind?

CHARNAU: Of course I can't see any at the moment, because there isn't any. That's what you're to look out for.
(*CARESME holds up a finger. He smells the air. He becomes disheartened.*)

CARESME: Nothing. There'll never be any wind. We've sailed beyond it. There'll never be any wind again.

CHARNAU: We haven't sailed beyond it. There will be wind again, I tell you. Keep watching.

CARESME: I can't go on. The wind has died forever. We're lost.

CHARNAU: We're not.

CARESME: We are.

CHARNAU: We're not. (*Hits CARESME.*)

CARESME: We're not.

CHARNAU: I told you we weren't.

CARESME: But there's still no wind.

CHARNAU: Well, in that case we'll have to make some.

CARESME: How?

CHARNAU: You can still breathe, can't you?

CARESME: Yes.

CHARNAU: You still have a set of lungs, don't you?

CARESME: Yes.

CHARNAU: Then blow.

CARESME: Blow?

CHARNAU: Blow. (*Begins beating him.*) Blow you good for nothing crewman! Blow helmsman, boatswain, blow all of you.

CARESME: What?

CHARNAU: Blow!

CARESME: Me?

CHARNAU: Yes you. West by south-west.

CARESME: What? (*He begins to blow through the beating.*)

CHARNAU: Blow, you good for nothing bastard!

CARESME: O God, I'm doing the best I can.

CHARNAU: That's not good enough for me.

CARESME: Have mercy on me.

CHARNAU: Mercy never made a penny. Blow, you lazy son of a bitch.

CARESME: But I'm fit to drop.

CHARNAU: Aren't we all? Blow man, blow.

(*CARESME collapses.*)

CARESME: We haven't moved an inch for all that work.

CHARNAU: You useless lump of flesh. You don't deserve to live.

CARESME: We're stuck here for ever.

(*Silence.*)

CHARNAU: I spy with my little eye, something beginning with *C.*

CHRISTOPHE: (*Bored.*) Caresme.

CHARNAU: Yes.

CARESME: I spy with my little eye, something beginning with... *C.*

CHRISTOPHE: Charnau.

CARESME: Yes.

CHARNAU: I spy with my little eye, something beginning with... *C.*

CARESME: Christophe.

CHARNAU: No. Yes. Only joking.

CHRISTOPHE: I spy with my little eye, something beginning with *S.*

CHARNAU: O, a novelty; sky?

CHRISTOPHE: No.

CARESME: Seagull?

CHRISTOPHE: No.

CHARNAU: We give up.

CHRISTOPHE: Sea.

(*Silence.*)

It wasn't meant to be like this.

(*Silence. CHARNAU sniffs the air.*)

CHARNAU: There is a bit of wind.

CHRISTOPHE: Not enough to blow these hulks.

CHARNAU: No. Perhaps not. But if we were a bit lighter.

(*CHARNAU nudges CHRISTOPHE. CHARNAU then approaches CARESME.*)

CHARNAU: The admiral, after due consultation with me, the ship's pilot, has decided that, in an attempt to streamline our industry and to enable our ships to move at a more competitive rate, to let the crew go, so to speak.

CARESME: What?

CHARNAU: You're to be made redundant.

CARESME: You mean I'm unemployed?

CHARNAU: Yes.

CARESME: So I can put my feet up for the rest of the journey?

CHARNAU: Metaphorically.

CARESME: ?

CHARNAU: Well as I'm sure you'll understand, we can't afford to have stowaways on board the ship so I'll have to ask you to leave.

CARESME: But where to?

CHARNAU: That's your affair.

CARESME: But I'll picket, I'll, protest, I'll form a union.

CHARNAU: A union of one? Bollocks.
(*CHARNAU thumps CARESME who falls overboard. CARESME flails about the auditorium, drowning.*)

CARESME: Help, I'm drowning. Save me please.

CHARNAU: I'm afraid we're not in a position to.

CARESME: Help me, for God's sake.

CHRISTOPHE: Let your God save you.

CHARNAU: Meet thy maker.

CHRISTOPHE: Ask him what grudge he has against us.

CARESME: Help me, help me please, I'm drowning. Save me Christophe.

CHRISTOPHE: Why should I save you when I can't even save myself?

CARESME: O God, I'm drowning, I'm dying, sinking. Please Christophe, I'm sink – I'm not sinking, I'm floating, I'm still alive. The water's thick, thick as land, thick as earth. I can... I can walk on water.

CHARNAU: What?
(*CARESME discovers he can run and dance on water, not to mention walk.*)

CARESME: A miracle, I'm saved. I can walk on water. Praise the Lord, a miracle.

CHARNAU: A miracle? (*He discovers a weed in the water.*) A weed.

CHRISTOPHE: Sargasso weed. That's it. Look, here on the map. 'A sea as thick as land lying between the old world and the new.' It must be a miracle. We have been moving, we just didn't realise it.

CARESME: A miracle, I can walk on water. (*He starts to drown again.*)

CARESME: I can – drown. Help me, I'm drowning. Save me, Christophe!

CHRISTOPHE: Get him out of the water.

CHARNAU: Save him?

CARESME: Help me –

CHRISTOPHE: Save him, Charnau.

CHARNAU: Why?

CHRISTOPHE: Because –

CHARNAU: Because what?

CHRISTOPHE: Because he's a man.

CHARNAU: Not a real man.

CHRISTOPHE: He's still a man.

CHARNAU: But he's dying.

CHRISTOPHE: He deserves to live as much as us.

CHARNAU: Why?

(*CHRISTOPHE ignores CHARNAU and pulls CARESME out.*)

You liberal!

CARESME: Thank you Christophe.

CHRISTOPHE: It's okay.

CARESME: I want to live, Christophe. I want to feel the grass beneath my feet and the sun on my back.

CHRISTOPHE: You shall.

CHARNAU: But when are we going to get there? Answer me that.

CHRISTOPHE: (*Map in hand.*) When? Three days. Give me three days.

CARESME: Three days and we shall be there.

CHARNAU: Or on the third day I shall rip you limb from limb.

Scene 12: The Farce

CARESME and CHARNAU are asleep. CHRISTOPHE rushes into INNOCENCE's arms.

CHRISTOPHE: You were right, a miracle!

INNOCENCE: A miracle?

CHRISTOPHE: He called me.

INNOCENCE: I knew you'd hear Christ's calling one day.

CHRISTOPHE: No, Caresme called me. 'Save me, Christophe, save me,' he called.

INNOCENCE: And Christ called you to save him.

CHRISTOPHE: He could walk on water, you see.

INNOCENCE: O, his ways are mysterious to men.

CHRISTOPHE: All I had to do was pull him out.

INNOCENCE: You saved a drowning man? You raised a Lazarus? O you healer of men. When I think of the pain you suffered, when I think of how I doubted you, I want hide myself away, far away from anybody. I want to fall into a river and be forgotten by the whole world. I want to pull out my eyes, my hair, rip off my head for the shame I feel. How can you forgive me for the wounds I have inflicted on you?

CHRISTOPHE: All I did was pull him out and I could feel a new world grow round me, fertile, rich and free.

INNOCENCE: O my chevalier.

CHRISTOPHE: My angel.

INNOCENCE: My beacon.

CHRISTOPHE: My soul's desire.

INNOCENCE: My world.

CHRISTOPHE: My America.

INNOCENCE: My Chistophe.

CHRISTOPHE: My new found land.

INNOCENCE: Take me to you, let me be yours.
    (*Pause.*)

CHRISTOPHE: Innocence?

INNOCENCE: Christophe?

CHRISTOPHE: Innocence?

INNOCENCE: Christophe?

CHRISTOPHE: I want –

INNOCENCE: Yes?

CHRISTOPHE: I want –

INNOCENCE: Yes?

CHRISTOPHE: I want to know him as you know him.

INNOCENCE: O. Yes. But you must know him.

CHRISTOPHE: But I only felt something of his goodness.

INNOCENCE: I felt good all over.

CHRISTOPHE: But I want to know what it was.

INNOCENCE: You have a vocation. A calling. That's all. Enough of such things.

CHRISTOPHE: But you have a vocation. Tell me about it.

INNOCENCE: I am not lucky enough to have a vocation. That is why I am destined to obey his teachings, to serve him as a humble nurse. Life on earth is a continual warfare, true peace of heart can only be found by resisting passions.

CHRISTOPHE: One must deny all passions and live for him.

INNOCENCE: (*Glum.*) Yes.

CHRISTOPHE: Deny lust.

INNOCENCE: Or you shall wallow in the flesh.

CHRISTOPHE: Deny good food.

INNOCENCE: Or you shall die of gluttony.

CHRISTOPHE: Yes, yes, deny it all, the sunshine, the desert, the sea.

INNOCENCE: Or you shall burn or parch or drown.

CHRISTOPHE: Deny life and love itself.

INNOCENCE: Yes, yes, resist it all – no. Not it all. Surely?

CHRISTOPHE: Then what passions don't we deny?

INNOCENCE: I cannot say. All is so transitory. So hard to grasp. (*A moment of enlightenment.*) I am left with nothing. I have nothing but you. (*She rips off her crucifix.*) Look, look, I cast it all off. Take me to you Christophe –

CHRISTOPHE: But you shall wallow in the flesh.

INNOCENCE: Let me wallow, let me wallow, let me gorge myself upon you.

CHRISTOPHE: You must resist passion.

INNOCENCE: Let me love you.

CHRISTOPHE: I can't.

INNOCENCE: You must or you shall plunge me into a blacker hole of despair than you could ever fathom.

CHRISTOPHE: O God, why did you do this to me – leave me, leave me be. (*He pushes her away from him.*)

INNOCENCE: Just when I thought I was finally – fuck.

Scene 13: New World

The three patients stand in their three boats.

CHRISTOPHE: Look!

CARESME: What?

CHRISTOPHE: Land ho!

CHARNAU: Where?

CHRISTOPHE: There. A light. Look! Like a candle flame rising and falling and rising again. I knew it was there all the time.

CHARNAU: Wealth! Riches! It must lie there!

CHRISTOPHE: Rush on.

CARESME: The world doesn't end. It's round, it's round. There's so much still to be discovered.

CHRISTOPHE: Pitch, roll through spray. Fly on.

CHARNAU: Trim the mainsail.

CHRISTOPHE: It looks like a dark green city built to nature. It shines like a luxurious jewel.

CHARNAU: Jasper, sapphire –

CARESME: Walls of trees. Dark doorways –

CHARNAU: Calcedony, emerald, onyx. Row me to them –

CHRISTOPHE: Birds and flowers of every colour. Scarlet, burgundy, gold –

CHARNAU: Gold. Gold and carnelia, beryl and topaz –

CARESME: We'll live and die with nature.

CHRISTOPHE: No, just live.

CHARNAU: I'll have you; jasper, amethyst, diamond. (*The boats hit land. Pause.*)

CHRISTOPHE: Land!

CHARNAU: Wealth!

CARESME: Salvador!

CHRISTOPHE: Gloria in excelsis.

(*CHARNAU and CARESME leap into the auditorium.*)

CHARNAU: Gold! Gold! There must be some around here.

(*CHARNAU rifles pesters audience members for money.*)

CHRISTOPHE: All this indescribable beauty. The golden world of which the writers of old speak.

CARESME: When I was young my grandfather sat me on his knee and told me of a miraculous land of plenty.

CHRISTOPHE: This is it, Caresme. This is it.

CHARNAU: Gold! Gold! I smell it! Dig!

(*CHARNAU starts digging.*)

CARESME: Sand, grass, sunshine, sea.

CHRISTOPHE: This is land where we can live in innocence, without force and laws and libel.

CHARNAU: I smell you. I'll have you. I'll buy and sell the world.

CHRISTOPHE: No more pain, Caresme, no more suffering, no more tears.

(*Chocolate money rains down on the audience.*)

CHARNAU: Gold! Gold! I've found it!

(*CHRISTOPHE and CARESME pick up some money and start to eat it. CHARNAU pulls a gun, toy or otherwise, and points it at the other two.*)

Put that down. Put that down I say, that's mine. Put it down I said. I've gold enough to buy and sell you all now. Admiral, crewmen; slaves!

(*The MATRON enters.*)

MATRON: These games have gone too far. Get back to bed, all of you. Move!

(*They do so. As they do so, she takes the map from CHRISTOPHE. CHARNAU hides his gun. The MATRON leaves.*)

CARESME: The map! Gone. New World, Christophe? You promised me a new world, but it's the same old stinking world. The same old stinking ward. Nothing changed; the matron, the nurses, the walls. O God, giver of breath, sway of the sea, drown me amongst your shoals.

CHRISTOPHE: It's here, and I'll prove it.

(*He runs towards light. He turns it off. Darkness.*)

CARESME: O God, I'm dead. Too soon. Too soon.

CHRISTOPHE: I'll show you all.

(*A ripping noise.*)

Scene 14: Denouement

Lights return. The MATRON is naked.

CARESME: I'm not dead. I'm alive. Matron!?

CHRISTOPHE: Look, we had the power to free ourselves all along.

MATRON: Christophe!

CHRISTOPHE: Matron?

MATRON: Christophe, we're so proud of you.

CHRISTOPHE: What?

MATRON: So proud of your achievements.

(*CHARNAU applauds vigorously, the others less energetically.*)

CHARNAU: Yes Matron.

MATRON: An example to us all, is he not friends?

CHARNAU: Yes, Matron.

MATRON: An example of fortitude, rectitude and attitude. He has struggled on with courage and valour and intelligence –

CHRISTOPHE: What are you doing?

MATRON: We are honouring you; because we are proud of you, because we love you, because you are now over us.

CHRISTOPHE: But I hate you –

MATRON: Sister, the medal.

(*SISTER INNOCENCE drags in a large lock and chain which she and the MATRON proceed to wrap around CHIRSTOPHE.*)

My friends, we are gathered here to honour a son of ours who has undertaken an arduous journey, charted and discovered new continents –

CARESME: But –

MATRON: We his friends welcome him back to our womb –

CHRISTOPHE: No! No!

MATRON: (*Enveloping him.*) The womb of the old world, the womb of order and reason, the womb of health and moral deceny, my womb. And without further ado I would like to present our brave admiral with this medal as a token of our esteem for his contribution to our society –

CHRISTOPHE: For society? For you, you mean. I'll get out of this.

CARESME: But how?

MATRON: Yes, how?

CHRISTOPHE: I'll tell you how.

(*He struggles free from the chain. Angelic music. Angelic light. A rope ladder drops.*)

MATRON: You'll stay right here, Christophe. You belong in the old world.

CHRISTOPHE: I'm leaving and I'm never coming back.

CHARNAU: O no you're not.

ALL: What?

CHARNAU: Hold the music.

(*Music ceases. CHARNAU produces his gun. He shoots CHIRSTOPHE. He goes to ladder.*)

Now I'm leaving and I'm never coming back.

CHRISTOPHE: You can't do this, tell him, Matron.

MATRON: You're so brave now, but you'll be afraid of what you might find.

CHARNAU: What could I find worse than myself? Maestro!

(*Music resumes.*)

INNOCENCE: Charnau, save me too.

CHRISTOPHE: Innocence!

MATRON: Your work! Your vocation, sister!

CHRISTOPHE: So it was you who she loved after all?

CHARNAU: Of course, mon capitaine. Come my ripened peach.

CHRISTOPHE: You heartless bastard.

CHARNAU: You snivelling fool.

INNOCENCE: O Charnau, I love you.

MATRON: And you on duty, sister.

CHARNAU: What about Caresme?

INNOCENCE: Bring him along, we'll need a slave. Move it!

(*The three ascend the ladder.*)

CHRISTOPHE: Caresme too?

MATRON: Come back, do you hear me?

CHRISTOPHE: They can't win like this, tell them they can't, Matron. It's not fair. It's cheating.

MATRON: Get back to bed! Get back to bed!

CHARNAU: So long suckers, good-bye cruel world!

CHRISTOPHE: Let's say au revoir.

CHARNAU: No, let's say good-bye.

MATRON: Get back to bed all of you!

(*Blackout. Music continues.*)

Scene 15: Trivial Pursuits

CHIRSTOPHE is hanging himself on his drip while the MATRON knits. They are playing Trivial Pursuit.

MATRON: It's your go.

CHRISTOPHE: O my God, why me?

MATRON: Because I just got my question wrong. It's your go.

CHRISTOPHE: What have I done to deserve this?

MATRON: Shake the dice.

CHRISTOPHE: (*Does so.*) Five.

MATRON: (*Moving his piece for him.*) One, two, three, four, five. Entertainment. Which Western star was known as the Duke?

CHRISTOPHE: John Wayne.

MATRON: There. What have you got to be so miserable about? You're winning.

CHRISTOPHE: Yes, I suppose I am.

MATRON: This will cheer you up: who shot John Wayne?

CHRISTOPHE: I don't know.

MATRON: Go on, have a guess.

CHRISTOPHE: I don't know.

MATRON: Go on.

CHRISTOPHE: No.

MATRON: Burt Lungcancer.

CHRISTOPHE: Don't say it. If it wasn't a word, then it mightn't exist.

MATRON: Nonsense, nonsense, it is a word, it does exist. Shake again. This is getting exciting, isn't it Christophe?

CHRISTOPHE: If you insist.

MATRON: I do.

CHRISTOPHE: Six.

MATRON: One, two, three, four, five, six. The History
   cheese. This to win. Who discovered the Americas?
CHRISTOPHE: Eh. Em. Ah. It's on the tip of my tongue.
MATRON: Any idea.
CHRISTOPHE: Charnau, ask Charnau. He had all the
   answers.
MATRON: Who?
CHRISTOPHE: He'll help me.
MATRON: Who will?
CHRISTOPHE: Charnau.
MATRON: Charnau who?
CHRISTOPHE: I don't know his surname. He was here, just
   a moment ago.
MATRON: There was no one here by that name.
CHRISTOPHE: There was. He was. But he's gone. Maybe he
   got better. Maybe he died.
MATRON: He must have died centuries ago or I'd know him.
   I know everyone here and at the moment there's only you.
CHARNAU: Centuries ago? He was here ten minutes ago.
MATRON: He was not.
CHRISTOPHE: He was too.
MATRON: You're imagining things.
CHRISTOPHE: I'm not, I tell you. He was really here.
MATRON: Real? How do you know what's real and what's
   not?
CHRISTOPHE: How do you?
MATRON: Don't be impertinent.
CHRISTOPHE: Don't twist the truth.
MATRON: Don't tell me what to do.
CHRISTOPHE: Don't tell me lies.
MATRON: Don't think you'll get away with this. That's the
   last game I play with you. Get back to what you were
   doing.
   (*MATRON leaves. CHIRSTOPHE resumes hanging
   himself.*)
CHRISTOPHE: O my God, why me? Matron? Who did
   discover the Americas? Who did discover the new world?

(*Silence.*)
Is there anyone there?

The End.

VINEGAR AND BROWN PAPER

for Ann O'Neill

Characters

JACK

JILL

MOTHER

Vinegar and Brown Paper was first performed by the Abbey Theatre Company at the Peacock Theatre, Dublin, 6 June 1995 with the following cast:

JACK, Stephen Kennedy

JILL, Clara Simpson

MOTHER, Fidelma Cullen

Director, Brian Brady

ACT ONE

The stage is in darkness. There is the sudden shocked 'Hunh' of someone waking from a nightmare. The lights slowly rise to a moonlit level to reveal in outline a sofa, a table, a chair, a door and a woman in her early to mid-thirties, who stands in her nightshirt. The light slowly rises in the course of the scene to a chilly early morning level.

JILL: What landscape's this? Ashen plain, ashen hills, ashen sky. No. Charcoal. Charcoal sky. There's a man. Steel grey shadow against ash and charcoal. Is standing as I do. Arms in similar ambiguous position. Grant it is position of divine sacrifice, but also suggests man poised to embrace...thin air. Been here before. Every time closed eyes. Mother, want to go home! Look again. (*Quoting.*) Eye is the window of soul, chief organ whereby understanding can be most complete. Perhaps this my soul?
(*Pause.*)
Describe; steel grey image of man in ashen landscape. Been here long time; Dawn twilight reveals dust of millennia upon shoulders. Good. Keep going. Seems more resigned than I. How say that with any certainty? Possibly be thinking? What difference? Words, weightless clouds. But need meaning, so decide. This man, in position not dissimilar to own, thinks – thinks about God. Wonders if God is there and if is he will save from this...predicament. And if is no God, wonders if has power to free self from past. Sheer hypothesis. Don't care. Not going to stay like this forever. In dark. Man in ashen landscape frightened and angry. Realising guilt if God be there, abandoned and alone if he be not. This man, Judas Iscariot, is raging across the centuries...
(*The lights have risen to an early morning level. There is a crash outside the door. JILL seems startled out of her dream. There is a muffled but audible 'Fuck'. JILL closes her eyes. JACK enters. He carries a box of painting equipment, easel and a large blank canvas. He stumbles in. Items tumble to the ground. He places the canvas at the back centre, then flops down in a chair.*)

JACK: Jesus Christ, I'm crucified with this load!
(*He awaits some reaction. Pause. There is none.*)
Thank you, thank you, you're too kind. It's great to be
back amongst my own people. There's that unique rapport,
there's that heart-felt appreciation, but most importantly,
there's that manifest love. Thank you. Thank you.
(*Pause.*)
Next!
(*Slumps down in a chair.*)
You awake?

JILL: Shhh. I'm thinking.

JACK: Well fuck that for a welcome. I cart your painting stuff
all the way from London –

JILL: Ssshhhh

JACK: Mother Ireland how are you! I'm on the next boat out
of here. (*Turns in jest to go.*)

JILL: It's all rubbish.

JACK: You can say that again. What is?

JILL: Everything. Everything I've done and said for the past
ten years. Rubbish like –

JACK: Like 'I love you, Jack, you're the funniest comic alive
– '

JILL: – like everything else in this plastic world.

JACK: Eight o'clock in the morning. I'm really not in the
mood –

JILL: People aren't living lives anymore, they're living
simulacra of lives shot at them from all sides, a virtual
reality of TV, Nintendo, karaoke, terriaki, nagasaki and
Dalai fucking Lamas – art should do something, shouldn't
it?

JACK: It should stay in bed till mid-day, at least.

JILL: It should explore the wasteland of the modern soul.

JACK: Isn't that what staying in bed till mid-day is all about?

JILL: The language of art has lost all relationship to the
world in which we're living. It's either mad self-reflexive
systems of signifiers signifying their own inability to signify
anything. Or kitsch reappropriations of expropriated
language. Look at me, for God sake.

JACK: I have eyes only for you.

JILL: My own language doesn't mean anything anymore.

JACK: You could say that again. Or could you?

JILL: That's why I ground to a halt in London.

JACK: I'm not surprised.

JILL: I couldn't be sure that things didn't mean anything anymore.

JACK: (*Lighting a cigarette.*) I don't quite catch you.

JILL: I'm not sure that I still believed in not being able to express anything anymore.

JACK: You're doing quite a good job now.
> (*JILL takes cigarette from him and extinguishes it.*)

JILL: I've had enough of art that tells us we're living second hand lives, speaking second hand languages, then takes the money and runs. Like Warhol, Koons and –

JACK: (*Imitating.*) We'll fix them damn coons good and proper. (*As himself. Bored.*) We've been here a hundred times before.

JILL: No we haven't, because this time I know what I'm going to do.

JACK: So do I. Tea, toast and a bowl of Kellogg's finest. (*He goes off left to where the kitchen is.*)

JILL: Throw out the designer aesthetics of to-day.

JACK: (*Off.*) What?

JILL: Go back to when the language of art was the means of signifying and understanding the artifice of God.

JACK: (*Off.*) What on earth?

JILL: Yes. On earth. The Renaissance ideal – to illuminate the light of God's creation on earth. Like the Dutch School.

JACK: (*Off.*) Got you. Total Football.

JILL: Hugo Van Der Goes, Pieter Breugal and Derryck Bouts.

JACK: (*Off.*) Johann Cryuff, the finest boots of all.

JILL: God's craftsmen.

JACK: (*Off.*) If there is a God, then Cryuff was one of his greatest. Ah Jesus, Jill, there's no bloody milk, and not a clean bowl in the house.
> (*JACK re-enters and roots through JILL's box.*)

JILL: There must be one.

JACK: Not one, all the buggers are filthy.

JILL: He can't die just like that.

JACK: You still on about that filthy bugger?

JILL: I'm beginning to think there is one, or, at least, there was one, but he abandoned us.

JACK: Where'd he go then?

JILL: I don't know. Perhaps he's in hiding.

JACK: I thought he was everywhere. Not many places left to hide.

JILL: But he will be back to beg our forgiveness, like a prodigal son. I found an old diary in mother's attic last week.

JACK: So you went back?

JILL: Yes.

JACK: How was it?

JILL: I don't want to talk about it.

JACK: Okay.

    (*Pause.*)

JILL: Hieronymous was lying dead on the kitchen floor, his legs stiff in the air, starved to death.

JACK: A bridge partner or one of the golf club crowd?

JILL: A cat.

JACK: What would the mother have said?

JILL: Don't. I just don't want to talk about it.

JACK: Okay.

    (*Pause.*)

JILL: I felt so guilty, and angry and –

JACK: Do you want to talk about it?

JILL: Listen Jack, I don't want to talk about it, okay?

JACK: Now I know we're home. I nearly miss the old boot. If she was still alive, we'd still be in London. No fear of you coming back with her still –

JILL: (*Ignoring him.*) In this diary I'd written; O God, if there is a God, save my soul, if I have a soul.

JACK: Did Hieronymous scribble that before he croaked it?

JILL: (*Archly.*) I think Augustine said that.

JACK: What band was he with?

JILL: Don't you see, that's what it all should be about.

JACK: I once found an old diary of mine and the only entry was: No future, no future. I'm pretty sure Johnny Rotten said that. And that's what it *is* all about for me, and most people in this godforsaken country. Was Augustine lead singer of The Damned?

JILL: And that's what I'm going to paint.

JACK: The Damned or the godforsaken island?

JILL: Both. The man God abandoned.

JACK: Which is my better side?

JILL: Judas.

JACK: (*Mock hurt.*) How dare you? I deserve better than this, after all I've done –

JILL: (*Goes to him.*) Jack!

JACK: Jill?

JILL: Jacko!

JACK: Gillian!

JILL: (*Smacking him lightly.*) Don't call me that. But thanks, anyway.

JACK: (*Dispirited.*) It was nothing.

JILL: (*Excited.*) I never thought I'd feel like this again.

JACK: Nor did I. Haven't felt this wrecked since I arrived in London nine years ago off the same tub and train and realised that the streets were paved with cardboard and not with gold. God I miss it. Let's go back.

JILL: It's going to be Judas' passion

JACK: And what about Jack's passion?

JILL: I saw this man, waiting and waiting, in this landscape of ashes; Judas Iscariot awaiting explanation from the God who had abandoned him.

JACK: Have you been taking your pills?

(*Pause.*)

Is that what this is all about, then?

JILL: I'm not alive when I'm taking them.

JACK: You want to kill yourself when you're not.

JILL: Not anymore. I want to work again.

JACK: So you've come back to Dublin to go on the dole.

JILL: The island of saints and scholars.

JACK: The island of stains and squalors.
> (*Without JILL seeing, JACK takes her pestle and mortar out of a box and goes to the kitchen. JILL goes to the boxes and starts going through them.*)

JILL: I was just pretending all that time in London.

JACK: (*Off.*) You mean you faked all those orgasms?

JILL: What are they? The more they paid me, the more important I thought myself, for telling them all how they would sell their own mothers for a few grubby pennies, and there I was…
> (*JACK re-enters with a mortar full of corn flakes and commences trying to eat them with the pestle. JILL starts sorting her paints into piles.*)

JACK: I quite liked the dollar bill tits with mirrored nipples. You should take your pills. You were off the rails without them. You didn't go out for months. Hiding under your duvet or sitting in front of the television all day. Australian soap operas? You weren't well.

JILL: I know, but –

JACK: Seriously, Jill, you couldn't handle things –

JILL: But the things have changed. I'm back to my old country and my old self.

JACK: What are you doing?

JILL: My renaissance.

JACK: But –

JILL: Most of this stuff is useless.

JACK: Then why did I have to go all the way to London to get it?

JILL: So I could see whether it would be of any use. I mean, look at this. (*She throws him a tube of paint.*)

JACK: (*Bends down to pick it up.*) What's wrong with it?

JILL: Prussian blue!

JACK: It can't help being German. No German can help being German.

JILL: An eighteenth-century invention. There is only one blue, the holy blue, the most expensive of all colours, made from ground lapis lazuli.

JACK: And I suppose you're going to buy that with your butter vouchers.

JILL: It was only used for the Virgin Mother's dress.

JACK: You're okay there, your mother always preferred
    polyester. Do you remember that time she came to stay
    and the electric fire –

JILL: Enough, Jack, I don't want to talk about it. I'll have no
    remembering in this house.

JACK: Flat.

JILL: Flat. Especially not of her. This is a new start.
    (*JILL keeps sorting through her things. JACK sees a letter
    on the floor.*)

JACK: (*Opening it.*) What's this?

JILL: (*Distractedly.*) It arrived for you yesterday…or the day
    before…sorry, I forgot…and a 'Fred from the Funny Club'
    was looking for you.

JACK: (*Shocked, reading the letter.*) Some remembering in this
    fucking flat mightn't go astray. This is a matter of life and
    death.

JILL: Is he in there for treatment?

JACK: Not everyone needs treatment. It's a bloody comedy
    club. I'm booked for a gig: Tuesday. Tomorrow!

JILL: That is funny.

JACK: Hilarious. My first gig in my home town. My first gig
    anywhere for that matter. How am I meant to stand up in
    front of a hundred people and make them laugh?

JILL: Tell them about my mother.

JACK: Mother-in-law jokes! Will I have a crack at 'queers' and
    'blacks' while I'm at it?

JILL: She seems to provide an endless source of amusement to
    you in private.

JACK: That's between you and me. Our own personal
    comedy.

JILL: My mother was sad not funny.

JACK: It's the way you tell 'em. (*Squatting down with head in
    hands.*) Think funny! Think funny! Think funny!

JILL: You do that already.

JACK: Ha-bloody-ha.

JILL: Where is my pestle and mortar? (*She sees the pestle and
    mortar and grabs it from JACK.*)

JACK: Not surprised they didn't eat cornflakes in the
    Renaissance with spoons like that.

JILL: I wish you'd be serious. This is important.

JACK: You wouldn't like me when I'm serious.

JILL: Why not?

JACK: Because I get angry when I'm serious.

JILL: About what?

    (*Pause.*)

JACK: 'About what'?

JILL: Yes, Jack, angry about what?

JACK: I'll tell you 'about what', Jill, or 'what about', as people like me say. Angry about having sweet f. all education or chance in life like you, angry about the five years of my precious youth spent labouring on the stinking sites of London. Angry that even this pathetic existence was taken from me when some rich bastards decided someone's got to pay for their boom and I'm that someone. Angry that I was expected to live on £32.50 a week, angry about drinking myself into oblivion so I wouldn't have to look at the rancid corner of world your God chose to illuminate for me, angry about the girl I...

JILL: What girl?

JACK: Doesn't matter.

JILL: Does to me.

JACK: Well, tough shit, I'm on a roll, not in a confessional. And though I am truly grateful to you for condescending to pick me out of the gutter, and I can on this occasion overlook the lack of welcome, milk for my corn flakes, clean bowl to put my corn flakes in and the fact that you keep banging on about God and art, because it is so long since I've seen you so excited about anything, I am really bloody angry that you did not think it of sufficient importance to remember to tell me that FRED FROM THE FUNNY CLUB HAS BOOKED ME FOR TONIGHT, WHEN I HAVE BEEN WAITING FOR A GIG LIKE THIS FOR TWO BLOODY YEARS. (*Calmly.*) That's 'about what' I'd be angry. But I'm not. Because I save my seriousness for my act so that I can be jocular Jake at home.

JILL: I'm not sure you're right.

JACK: WHAT ABOUT?

JILL: I quite like you when you're serious.
>   (*Pause.*)
>   You have a smouldering animality

JACK: (*Lights cigarette.*) Woof!
>   (*She runs a hand through his hair.*)
>   Stop it, I'm thinking

JILL: I could fall for you. (*She falls on his lap. Takes cigarette from him and extinguishes it.*)

JACK: You bitch!

JILL: You boor.

JACK: You tosser.

JILL: You turd.

JACK: You slut.

JILL: You scum.

JACK: You artist!

JILL: You critic!

JACK: I guess I'll have to shaft you now, just for the hell of it.
>   (*JILL feels his crotch. Childish voices.*)

JILL: Jack!

JACK: Jill?

JILL: You've a little hill.

JACK: And it ain't a pail of water.

JILL: Will Jill go down –
>   (*JILL starts to remove JACK's clothes. He wears cycling shorts and a vest underneath.*)

JACK: And Jack'll come crumbling after. (*Snorkelling.*)
>   Mmmmmm.
>   (*Pregnant pause.*)

JACK: (*Moaning.*) Aw, Jill!

JILL: Huh?

JACK: What about my routine…what am I going to say?

JILL: (*Looks up.*) Illuminate the world of the man God abandoned. (*She returns to his crotch.*)

JACK: (*Crumbling.*) This is getting nowhere fast… I've got to sign on…story of my life.

(*Loud grunge music. JACK jumps up, startled. He rapidly arranges a baseball cap on his head, takes a few deep breaths, then JACK explodes into his routine.*)

(*Sings/roars.*) Looked at my future,
Looked at my past,
Come to the conclusion
I'm going nowhere fast.
Going nowhere fast,
Going nowhere fast.
NEXT, NEXT, NEXT.

(*The music stops abruptly.*)

Just one of my turns. Story of my life. Been here, been there, been nowhere. Crouch End. The arsehole of nowhere. But I went there fast. As fast as a couple of milligrams of speed would allow. The English...what can you say? How about: BUNCH OF RACIST BASTARDS!

(*Blast of music.*)

(*Sings/roars.*) Mother Ireland you betrayed me
So I sailed for London Town,
Where I sold you up the river
With a girl...

(*Music stops.*)

This is getting nowhere fast. But seriously, it's good to be back. Went to see all my old friends to-day. Down the Labour Exchange. Labour Exchange, that's a good one. Wonder who thought that one up. Anyway, there they were, all my old friends in their little cages. The nowhere men. And women. Sitting in the nowhere land. And they got there a lot faster than I did. Good on them. 'I'm back' I said. But nobody was nowhere near. 'Did you miss me?' Nothing. 'I would like to exchange my labour for four pages of personal questions and an amount of money slightly but significantly under the basic rate of subsistence in this country.' Nothing. The nowhere gang were happy to sit at their desks in splendid desolation. Twenty minutes I wait. I thought this country cherished it's children. Isn't that what SPUC is all about. The society for the protection of the unemployed children. I thought they would rush to greet me with open arms. But no. I begin to feel a bit upset.

Is this any way to treat a lost son? Where is the fatted calf? Where my share of the inheritance in the first place? I wonder, not unreasonably. As I am asking myself these questions I begin to knock my head on the noise-proof, knacker-proof, nutter-proof glass. I like the sensation. (*He starts to butt and kick and make faces against the imaginary glass.*) It seems to sum up my life. I hit it a bit harder. Feels good. Start moaning. Feels even better. And before I know it, I'm having one of my turns.

(*Music starts.*)

(*Sings/roars.*)Looked at my future,

Looked at my past,

Come to the conclusion,

I'm getting nowhere fast.

NEXT, NEXT, NEXT.

(*Music and JACK stop abruptly.*)

Comic turns they are.

(*Does a completely silent version of the head-butting, kicking and face-making against the glass.*)

NEXT, a nowhere person says. I am plucked from my reverie and come to my senselessness, not to mention theirs. (*Plays the person behind desk too.*) Name? (*Mouths his name, soundlessly.*) Age? (*Ditto.*) Marital Status? (*Ditto.*) You see, their glass protects them not only from noise, knackers and nutters, it also protects them from information. Where have you been? Nowhere. Why did you return? I was getting nowhere, I say, stands to reason, if either of us had any. (*Makes face.*) Occupation? Comedian, I say. Could you repeat that? COMEDIAN,

I repeat. She heard that one. This is no place for joking! You see, I say, I must be a comedian. This is a serious matter, she says. So is comedy, I say, I would have been a tragic character, but as you are no doubt aware from your in-depth knowledge of twentieth-century aesthetics, in the absence of God or any absolute system of morality, there is no longer the potential for tragic action, since man's attempts at heroic action in a world that has no meaning are themselves ultimately meaningless and comically futile.

It was. NEXT, NEXT, NEXT.
(*Sings/roars.*) Mother Ireland you betrayed me,
So I sailed for London Town,
Where I sold you up the river,
With a girl…
Just one of my turns.
(*Music. Dances off in same manner as he entered. Blackout.*)

End of Act One.

ACT TWO

In the darkness the sudden sharp 'Hunh' of someone waking from a nightmare is heard. Lights come up in moonlit greys, blues and silver to reveal JILL.

JILL: Longer one spends in darkness, the clearer one sees manifold contrasts. Cinder path emerges from ash. Progress of a tear. A Via Dolorosa. Must begin. Or never reconcile. Station one: Judas pleads his case before his God. He argues: Listen to me whoever or wherever you are. I know you and all men shall vilify me; they will say I acted out of greed. Or that I was possessed by evil. Or that I was the terrorist with my own political agenda. But those who say that will say such things only because they will refuse to recognise themselves in me. Is it not more simple than that? Why does anyone act contrary to what they know to be right? Fear. I doubted you. Your existence, your presence, your love. And from that sprang fear. Fear and confusion. Fear of confusion. Fear of abandonment. I betrayed you because I feared you had abandoned me. And in my fear, I was blown like a leaf in the wind by the mumblings of Pharisee and zealot – Are you there? Does anyone hear me? I am only trying to explain. I am only beginning to see clearly, myself –don't leave me in the dark. (*Hurriedly.*) The kiss, you see, there was fear and confusion, betrayal and love. Don't leave me in the dark like this!
(*Pause.*)
Station two: out of the light of God, Judas accepts his cross and commences the path.
(*Beat.*)
Someone's there. Always there judging me from security of dark. Can feel the silent righteousness. Move on. Burden, like problem, seems larger in dark. Cannot see dimensions. Must rest.
(*Beat.*)

Who is it? Who's following me? Must keep going for fear, for fear, for fear the dark, for fear the dark sees, for fear the dark enters. Am sinking under the weight. Station three: Judas falls a first time. (*She falls.*) No-one there. Will voice come no more? Must I always fall?

(*Pause. Lights return to daytime. JACK enters, he carries a brown paper bag and he is whistling.*)

JACK: (*Cheerful, performance mode.*) Did you hear the one about the Irish joke...

(*Long pause.*)

That was it. The punchline. Do you think my public misses my subtle ironies, or is it just a bit shite? Jill? You there? (*Sees her.*) Well, what d'you think? Hit or miss?

(*No reply. JACK lights up a cigarette.*)

Next! Got one right up your street. Jesus, on the cross. Just about to croak it. Calls for Judas. 'Judas, come here, there's something I've got to say to you.'

JILL: (*Disinterestedly supplying the punchline.*) You dirty two-faced bastard.

JACK: (*Lamely, head-butts the air.*) Take that! Bit shite as well.

JILL: You've never worried what your audience thought before.

JACK: Didn't have an audience before. As Fred says, you've got to go with the flow if your career's going to grow. Wait till I tell you what he was telling me –

JILL: I wish you wouldn't smoke.

JACK: (*Puts out cigarette.*) What's up with you. *You* look a bit shite.

JILL: Thanks. I was overcome by my passion.

JACK: You should see someone.

JILL: How do you know I haven't been seeing someone?

JACK: Visions of crucified men is all you've been seeing.

JILL: Maybe I should spend a few weeks at the Funny Club, have Fred fix my head.

JACK: You're not well.

JILL: Poor Hieronymous.

JACK: What?

JILL: The cat.

JACK: What about him?

JILL: I keep remembering him.

JACK: What was that you said about remembering in this house?

JILL: Flat!

JACK: Damn, it's gone.

JILL: On the kitchen floor with his legs in the air staring at me accusingly

JACK: I could use that. The sad and lonely death of Hieronymous the cat. Listen, Fred was telling me –

JILL: I'm trying to be serious with you.

JACK: Well then, I will try to be serious. What, Jill, the fuck is wrong with you?

JILL: I thought you got angry when you got serious.

JACK: If I concentrate really hard, I can sometimes squeeze an ounce of concern out of my callous heart. Why don't you go out anymore?

JILL: I sign on.

JACK: Except to sign on.

JILL: What else is there to go out for?

JACK: Air?

JILL: In this city?

JACK: Well, what about your work then?

JILL: What about it?

JACK: You haven't done any.

JILL: It's not working like I thought it would. The more I think about this piece, the more I think it's not about what it seems to be about.

JACK: Not the brain busters again. What about your Renaissance thing?

JILL: They worked in the light of God. I'm working in the dark. I strive for the certainties of that world, but in mine nothing is sure. Everything in this world is plastic, malleable. In their world meaning was carved in granite. When Van Der Goes doubted his ability to illuminate his world, he could retire to a monastery. He could pass his last years in the light of God. Where can I go? The dole office?

JACK: I thought he became manager of Ajax Amsterdam.

JILL: Won't you understand anything? I don't really know what I'm doing anymore.

JACK: Well, I know what I'm doing. (*He takes out of the brown paper bag a new bowl, a new spoon, a box of cornflakes and a carton of milk.*) A bowl of Mr Kellogg's matchless flakes. Listen till I tell you what Fred was telling me –

(*JILL turns on the television. There are two remote controls. JACK turns the volume down, JILL turns it up.*)

I thought you hated television.

JILL: Ssssh.

JACK: I thought it was second-hand life. A plastic simulacra of life.

JILL: Simulacrum.

JACK: Or some crap like that. The last refuge of lost souls.

JILL: Okay, I admit it, Mother, I'm a lost soul. Now shut up. (*She turns up the sound.*)

(*The television intercuts the dialogue. It is an Australian soap opera.*)

JACK: Jill, for God's sake, I have been trying to tell you what Fred was telling me this morning.

JIM: (*On television.*) – what Frank was telling me –

JAN: (*On television.*) – what did he say, Jim – ?

JILL: Well?

JACK: He said…

JIM: (*On television.*) – he said he thinks I've got what it takes –

JACK: He thinks the act is coming on, he thinks I've got what it takes and, wait till you hear this, he thinks he can get me a supporting slot to Brendan Grace, if I make a few changes. (*Pause.*)

JIM: (*On television.*) – Frank thinks I'll make it –

JILL: And when you've made it you look like a dollar bill tit with a mirrored nipple. Anyway, who's Brendan Grace?

JACK: Don't know, but Fred says he's big. About eighteen stone.

JIM: (*On television.*) – he thinks I've got a big future in breakfast cereals.

JILL: What changes does Fred suggest?

JACK: He just thinks I've got to be a little more accessible if I want to succeed.

JIM: (*On television.*) – but I'm afraid I'm going to be less
    accessible, Jan –

JILL: What's more accessible.

JACK: Less stuff about the unemployed, you know.

JILL: That's the most accessible joke in this country.

JAN: (*On television.*) – what do you mean, less accessible, Jim?
    You can't leave me here on my own –

JACK: Unemployed ain't got no money.

JIM: (*On television.*) – I'm sick of being unemployed, sick of
    having no money.

JILL: What's it to be, Mother-in-law jokes?

JAN: (*On television.*) – what about my Mother? –

JILL: My Mother-in-law hates me so much she had a daughter
    for the sole purpose of making my life a misery.

JIM: (*On television.*) – your mother's making life a misery –

JACK: Jill, I'm not selling out. But what's the point in being a
    comedian if you never get a chance to perform?

JILL: What's the point in performing comedy if it isn't funny?

JACK: That's the tragedy of comedy.

JILL: And I suppose I'm the comedy of tragedy.

JIM: (*On television.*) What's the point in living like this?

JAN: (*On television.*) What's the point in living like that? It's the
    story of our lives.

JACK: Jill, do we have to have this on?

JILL: I like it. It's so true to life. A jumble of signifiers
    signifying nothing.

JIM: (*On television.*) What's that supposed to mean?

JACK: Listen Jill, it is necessary to be appreciated sometimes,
    just to keep faith in yourself.

JILL: I wouldn't know.

JAN: (*On television. Sobbing.*) – what about my mother?

JACK: I wish she'd shut up about her mother.

JIM: (*On television.*) – I wish you'd shut up about your
    mother…

JILL: I don't want to talk about my mother. It isn't my fault –

JACK: What isn't? Who said anything about your mother?

JILL: Nothing.

JACK: Listen, Jill, this is my life.

JILL: I had one of them once. It's just a phase, you'll soon grow out of it.

JIM: (*On television.*) Jan?

JACK: Jill!

JILL: Jack!

JAN: (*On television.*) Jim? Don't leave me. What are you thinking, Jim?

JIM: (*On television.*) I'm thinking, I'm sorry, I was only thinking of myself. I love you no matter what.

JAN: (*On television.*) I was only thinking of myself too. I love you too, Jim.

(*Pause. Romantic music signalling the end of the programme.*)

JACK: Jesus, will you turn that thing off. I can't hear myself think.

JILL: I can hear what you're thinking. You're thinking me, me, me.

JACK: And what the hell is wrong with you, you, you?

JILL: I'm fucking lost, that's what's wrong. Things should be different now, but I feel like I'm back to where I was in London. Was going to sort myself out. But so dark and lonely here, afraid, like Van der Goes, never hear the voice again, whose, don't know anymore, but the voice that comes when, when the child is afraid of dark, saying: 'it's okay, I'm here'.

JACK: It's okay, I'm here.

JILL: It's not the same. It comes from inside. Something I have to fix.

JACK: (*Gently.*) You should see a doctor. Maybe there are other pills, pills that don't –

JILL: I don't want any fucking pills. I want, I want, I want to be myself again, whatever that is, I want to believe.

VOICE-OVER: (*From television.*) Can Jan and Jim sort out their problems. Find out in next week's thrilling episode.

(*Blackout. The sudden shocked 'Hunh' of someone waking from a nightmare.*)

JILL: On. No choice now. (*Wearily.*) Station four: on the road to damnation Judas Iscariot encounters –

(*Long pause as JILL watchers her MOTHER enter. She is an imposing middle-class Dublin woman. She wears a blue polyester dress.*)

– his mother. What are you doing here?

MOTHER: That's a fine welcome after all these years. Living the high-life in London, forgetting your poor old grey-haired Irish mother.

JILL: You're neither poor, old, nor grey haired, Mother.

MOTHER: No, but I am a dead mother and that must qualify me for some form of martyrdom. Stand up straight, Gillian.

JILL: I can't. And don't call me that.

MOTHER: Why not? It's what I've always called you!

JILL: Exactly. Please, Mother, I don't have time– I'm trying to work.

MOTHER: Is that what you call it? Is this what you were too busy doing while I was wasting away in the hospice? I suppose I should count myself lucky you managed to squeeze in my funeral. O, I know all about it. Don't think I don't. Always knew more than I let on.

JILL: It was you watching me from the dark. Wasn't it? I don't want to be remembering this.

MOTHER: You think I want you to be? I've got better things to be doing with my time than standing around looking at you make a spectacle of yourself. I have a bridge appointment.

JILL: You haven't changed –

MOTHER: As if you'd notice if I had, but don't worry about me, you never did anyway.

JILL: O God, make her stop.

MOTHER: No use asking for his help. You stopped listening to him, like you stopped listening to your father, a long time ago.

JILL: Like my father, he never said anything to me.
(*MOTHER is looking around.*)
Are *you* listening to *me?*

MOTHER: (*Picking up dirty bowl of cornflakes.*) The state of this place. Maybe you weren't doing so well in London after all.

JILL: I was doing fine. I just couldn't stand it anymore. It wasn't me.

MOTHER: Those dungarees certainly aren't you. I always thought you looked better in a dress.

JILL: Just don't criticise me, Mother. I can't stand it when you criticise me.

MOTHER: A nice blue dress.

JILL: Lapis Lazuli.

MOTHER: Pardon?

JILL: You wouldn't understand.

MOTHER: Of course, I never understood anything. I never understand why we wasted all that money on your education, when all you wanted to do was live in a slum and draw pictures. You should have been a teacher, then nothing like this would have happened. What would your father say if he were here?

JILL: Nothing.

MOTHER: You were our only child. Won't you understand. We invested all our hope in you.

JILL: But that's exactly it. That's exactly why. Listen, if you must be here at least let me explain.

MOTHER: You should have done that years ago. When I had time. I am quite out of it now. Time that is. I've kept the bridge circle waiting long enough as it is. Good-bye Gillian. (*She starts to leave.*)

JILL: Let me explain, Mother!
(*MOTHER is gone. Pause.*)
Station five: Simon of Cyrene helps Judas.
(*MOTHER re-enters.*)

MOTHER: Simon of Cyrene indeed. I suppose he's one of your coloured friends from London. No, it's just me you'll meet about these parts.

JILL: Mother, if you won't let me explain then please, leave me in peace.

MOTHER: Indeed, isn't it me who's meant to be resting in peace. But don't worry, I'll be gone in a minute. I just thought, seeing as you were here, I'd ask you how Hieronymous was?
(*Pause.*)

JILL: Hieronymous? Mother, He's –

MOTHER: (*Seeing her carrying the canvas.*) Goodness, what's this you're carrying? Let me hold it for you. You're perspiring too –

JILL: Six: Veronica wipes the damned face.

(*MOTHER takes a lacey handkerchief from her handbag and wipes her face.*)

MOTHER: Veronica indeed. Have you forgotten your Mother's own name. May. Only film stars were called Veronica in my day. Everyone else was called May.

JILL: Mother please, I'm trying to work.

MOTHER: Are they paying you for it?

JILL: £59.20 a week plus butter vouchers.

MOTHER: What kind of wage is that?

JILL: The wage of sin. Theirs.

MOTHER: There we go, love, you look a bit better. (*She gives JILL back her canvas.*) And what were you saying about Hieronymous?

JILL: He's – I'm looking after him well, mother. He's fine. Never been better.

MOTHER: At least there's one thing you're doing well. (*Looks at watch.*) I'm so late. They'll kill me for keeping them waiting.

JILL: Mother, you *are* dead.

MOTHER: So I am. Still, I must rush. I'll tell them I was giving my daughter career advice. I tell them you work in the London market, you know.

JILL: Cattle market?

MOTHER: Goodness, no. The stock market. Can't let the side down, you know. Though I know you do your best to. (*She makes to leave.*) Good-bye Gillian.

JILL: Mother!

(*She's gone.*)

I hate you, I hate you, I hate you, I hate you, I hate you.

(*Beat.*)

Judas begins to think perhaps not entirely to blame. Thinks to himself: God made me, God knows all, therefore chose me to betray his son. Saw my weakness and exploited it.

Why did he not try to save me? Am I not son of man too? Why not save me? Why not save me? Am going mad. Who's who? Who's creator, who's created? Who's betrayer, who's betrayed? Station seven: Judas, myself, falls a second time.

(*She falls but remains where she is. Lights switch to JACK's performing spotlight. He enters, wearing a spangly silver suit, to the sound of canned applause. Each punchline is accompanied by canned laughter in this section.*)

JACK: Excuse me. One of my turns. Just got back from England. Still haven't fully recovered. I mean, the English, what can you say? How about: BUNCH OF RACIST BASTARDS!

(*Canned murmuring. He's thrown slightly.*)

I sometimes fear my audience miss my subtle ironies. Maybe I don't use enough starch.

(*One person laughs.*)

But you've got to admit it, the English do things differently.

(*Singular canned shriek.*)

She obviously knows what I mean; just lie back and think of England, Missus. That'll soon calm you down.

(*Canned laughter.*)

But seriously, poor Paddy has to watch his mouth over there. The things that come out of it, not to mention go into it…

(*Canned murmur.*)

(*Hesitant.*) I… I was at this disco and I said to this bloke 'What's the crack?'

(*Canned laughter.*)

And he turns to me and says (*Mincing.*) 'That's for you to know and me to find out, big boy?' (*Makes a face.*)

(*Canned laughter.*)

At this party once with my friend Rastos – a gentleman with a good tan, if you know what I mean –

(*Canned laughter.*)

'Ow's de crack, Mon?' he says. 'The crack's ninety,' says I. 'Mon, you was ripped off, I get mine for quarter de price.'

(*Canned murmuring. Pause.*)

After nine years there, I realise England's cracking up, and it's not at my jokes – they've got too much starch – so I return home to Ireland. First day back I go to the Labour Exchange. Labour exchange, that's a good one, wonder who thought that up.

(*Canned murmuring. Makes a decision. Starts with energy.*)

Anyway, you know what coming home means? Relations. Mine are alright. They're dead. But the girlfriend's mother! That's why I went to England in the first place, to get a divorce. From the mother-in-law. The mother-out-law, actually. At least, if she isn't out-lawed, she should be. I live in sin with her daughter. I know it's a sin, but someone's got to do it. Women, eh? You can't live with them, you can't live without them. But someone's got to do the ironies.

(*Canned laughter, applause.*)

(*To black.*)

COMPERE: (*Voice over.*) And now the act you've all been waiting for –

End of Act Two.

ACT THREE

The light rises on JACK and JILL who are having sex on the sofa in front of the television. It is a joyless act. Pushing, pulling, hitting and biting without passion. JACK has most of his clothes off and some of JILL's when JILL reaches for the remote control, turns the sound up and pushes him off. Without speaking to each other they react variously to the television drama and their own crumbling relationship.

VOICE-OVER: (*From television.*) And welcome back to the concluding part of our drama from down under.

JIM: (*On television.*) That was short and sweet.

JAN: (*On television.*) I wouldn't go so far as sweet.
(*Pause.*)

JIM: (*On television.*) Jan, we don't talk anymore.

JAN: (*On television.*) Yes we do, Jim. You said that was short and sweet and I said –

JIM: (*On television.*) We don't talk really.
(*JACK and JILL steal glances at each other.*)

JAN: (*On television.*) What's there to say, really? It seems like we spend all our time clambering up the same old hill only to tumble back down again. What's the point in trying anymore?
(*JACK sits down and lights up a cigarette. JILL looks at him.*)

JILL: I wish you wouldn't smoke.
(*JACK scowls at JILL and puts out the cigarette. Pause. JACK pours himself a bowl of cornflakes and starts eating glumly.*)

JIM: (*On television.*) This is the biggest day of my life, why can't you be happy for me?

JAN: (*On television.*) What about the day you met me? Was that not a big day?

JIM: (*On television.*) You know what I mean.

JAN: (*On television.*) I'm not sure I do, anymore. You've changed. You used to believe in something and now, and now your whole life revolves around, around breakfast cereals and that awful suit.

(*JACK looks at his bowl of cornflakes. He's in two minds.*)

JIM: (*On television.*) I had ideals, but I was getting nowhere. Now I've got a product people want to buy.

(*JACK continues eating his cornflakes.*)

JAN: (*On television.*) I sometimes think you love your breakfast cereals more than you love me.

(*JACK looks up, puts down bowl and rubs his hand.*)

JIM: (*On television.*) I don't have time for this. I've got to get ready.

(*Pause.*)

JAN: (*On television.*) It wasn't always like this.

JIM: (*On television.*) No.

JAN: (*On television.*) You used to make me laugh.

(*JACK and JILL look at each other.*)

JIM: (*On television.*) I could still make you laugh, if I wanted to.

JAN: (*On television.*) No you couldn't. Your jokes aren't funny anymore.

(*JACK looks suddenly furious then goes for his coat.*)

You leaving?

JIM: (*On television.*) Yeah. You coming with me or staying here?

JAN: (*On television.*) I'm staying. I came back to sort things out. I'm not giving up yet.

(*JACK goes to the door.*)

JIM: (*On television.*) You're not well. You should see someone.

JAN: (*On television.*) Maybe I've got to see less of someone.

JIM: (*On television.*) Happy to oblige. Don't expect me back.

(*JACK goes out and slams the door. A door slams on the TV. Pause.*)

JAN: (*On television.*) You'll be back. We all come back. Just like a criminal can't help returning to the scene of a crime.

(*Pause.*)

JILL: Jesus, what a cliched scene.

(*Romantic music signifying end of programme. Lights fade to blackout on JILL. There is the sudden shocked 'Hunh' of someone waking from a nightmare. Lights come on at moonlit dream level.*)

Way becomes clear only at end.

(*TV flicks on. Screen is visible to audience. An empty television studio stage.*)

VOICE-OVER: (*From television.*) – proudly introduce –

JILL: Have feared the light and what it might illuminate. Till now.

VOICE-OVER: (*From television.*) – talented young comic Jack-the-lad –

(*Canned applause. JACK appears. Pulls face. JACK on screen and JILL on stage both bow.*)

JACK: (*On television.*) Just one of my turns –
(*Canned laughter.*)

JILL: Station eight: you will not weep for me, women of Jerusalem, I know that, because I am what I am, and what you are, a Judas not a Jesus, a confused betrayer of love, not an object of pity. I doubted, I abandoned and I betrayed, like you have done to me but was I too not abandoned?
(*Pause.*)
No, you will not weep for me, women of Jerusalem, you will not listen to me, you will fail to see anything of yourselves in me.

JACK: (*On television.*) – forgive me, says the Mother-in-law, and the priest says, Say one Hail Mary and three how's your father's –
(*Canned laughter.*)

JILL: Station nine: fall a third time. (*She falls.*) No matter. Fall a forth, fifth, sixth time. Been falling down all my life. Used to it by now. But I will see this judgement lift from me.

JACK: (*On television. With less enthusiasm.*) – and the Mother-in-law has the padre in a half nelson. Bless me Mother, for I have sinned, he gasps. Indeed you have, says she –
(*Deafening canned laughter.*)

JILL: Station ten: rejoice, the moment is at hand. (*Taking off clothes.*) Become own model. Self portrait.

JACK: (*On television.*) – but the priest's attention has been caught by something –

JILL: (*Starts nailing her feet to canvas, in earnest.*) Eleven: On. Voice shall come, and voice shall say is all right, am here, am so sorry for leaving you on this hill to suffer, and shall

be no need to fear dark no more. (*She nails left wrist to canvas holding nail in left hand and hammer in the right.*) And shall have meaning –
(*She tries but obviously cannot put a nail into her right wrist. she tries a few times then gives up. Pause. She starts to laugh.*)
No-one there. Never will be. Abandoned. Self portrait as clown all that is possible. Now.

JACK: (*On television.*) ... Excuse me, says the priest, half choked, but I cannot help noticing that your pussy is dead. (*Canned laughter.*)
– and the priest takes her pussy in his hands –
(*Hysterical canned laughter.*)
(*JACK grows serious.*) Why are you laughing? It's not funny. Have you no self-respect? It's rubbish. Everything I've done and said for the past ten minutes. Jesus, have I no self-respect? Going nowhere fast all my life.
(*Without music he does his manic dance and sings/roars.*)
Looked at my future
Looked at my past
Come to the conclusion
I'm going nowhere fast.
You want to laugh? Try this one. It's a cracker. Living in London, right. Fallen to the bottom of the Primrose Hill with a clatter. One day wake up to find myself in the gutter, DTs in cardboard city, and there was this girl, sixteen at the most, sleeping rough. I try to talk to her because I'm shivering with, with the sickness of myself, and she's frightened. She won't say anything at first. What's your name? I says. Nothing. You don't have to tell me your real name, any name will do. Just talk to me. I wait. Mary, she says in this accent, my accent, Mary Magdalena. Jill would like that. Where are you from? I says. She won't look at me. I'm trying to get a better look at her face but I'm shaking something rotten, and I'm seeing other things. Where are you from, Mary? Ireland, she says. I kind of worked that one out. What part? I says. Dublin. Still she won't look at me. (*Raising voice, becoming threatening.*) What part of Dublin, Mary?

I says. Irishtown, Jack, she says and looks at me, Irishtown Jack Murphy. I don't remember her name, but the face, I see a little girl in pigtails playing at skipping on my road, but I am trembling now, what have we done to be abandoned like this, I'm thinking, alone and shivering, what have I done to deserve this? What the fuck are you doing here? I says to her, what the fuck are you doing living like this? And she is trying to say what the fuck are you doing, Jack Murphy? But you see, in my shaking and my shaking and the pictures in my head, I am smacking out at her and everything. And when the pictures stop I see that I've beaten the poor girl black and blue and senseless as myself.

(*Pause.*)

What the fuck am I doing here? (*Laughs hollowly.*) Just one of my turns.

(*JACK exits. JILL remains upon her cross. She is sleeping or unconscious. A strong shaft of light starts to appear. MOTHER enters but she is radically altered. Everything about her is altered and older.*)

MOTHER: Where are they? I've been looking and looking, for years it seems, but I just can't find them. They must have switched venues and no-one told me. No-one tells me anything and now they'll start without me.

JILL: (*Weakly.*) Mother?

MOTHER: I was so looking forward to it. I just couldn't find…my hair brush. (*She tries to comb her hair with her hand but a handful of it comes away.*)

JILL: Mother, what's happened to you? This isn't how I remember you, you've changed so –

MOTHER: Looking forward to one last bridge night before – my teeth don't fit me anymore. I'm coming apart at the seams.

JILL: But what is wrong?

MOTHER: Time. What is happening to time in this place? What is happening to me? I'm accelerating out of memory. It seems like only a moment ago I was talking to you in the prime of my life and you a headstrong young thing with all the world before you, just as a moment before that my own

mother was talking to me and I the same as you. Perhaps you are me, and I my own mother. A horrific thought. Or my own daughter. I'm so confused, Jill, I'm so lost.
(*Pause.*)

JILL: You called me Jill, Mother.

MOTHER: I hope I don't miss the game entirely. And my teeth, what about my teeth? You don't have any blu-tack, do you, love?
(*Pause. MOTHER looks at her properly for the first time.*)
Are you having problems there, love? (*Chuckles.*) You always struggled with your faith. Here, let me help you. I only ever wanted to help, you know.
(*MOTHER hammers in the last nail.*)
There. That's better. I'm quite puffed. But I've got to keep searching.

JILL: Hieronymous died, mother. I didn't look after him.

MOTHER: I thought as much. I was sure I saw him here a moment ago. But it's for the best. It'll be company. Your father still doesn't say very much. But I can't miss the game. Where are they? I've been looking and looking. They must have switched venues, and no-one told me. No-one tells me anything anymore. and now they'll have started without me. (*She starts to shuffle off.*)

JILL: Mother!
(*MOTHER leaves.*)
Mummy?
(*Dawn lights. Sun rising.*)
What landscape's this? Plains and hills radiating amber, ochre and apricot under golden sky. No, marmalade. There's a man standing as I do. Grant it is position of divine sacrifice, but also suggests a willingness to embrace everything. The light has returned and man is looking to light, as I do, and smiling as I do, because a voice is saying, 'it's okay, I'm here, forgive me for leaving you so long like this'. And Judas is climbing down off cross and is embracing the light. He has suffered enough.

The End.